aonghas macneacail

lia fàil

1

An cuala sibh an fhàilte bh'ann!
làn phandamóinidheam de dh'àigh!
a *Chlach* a tilleadh thar nan crìoch
gus laighe tiamhaidh mar bu chòir,
an tasgadh buan n h-albainn!
is sinne rinn an othail, o
is sinne rinn an othail!

2

theirte gur i bha siud, cho fada 'sa bheàrn fhuar
eadar ùrlar agus tòin righreachd (cho fada, cho fada air falbh),
their càch gu robh i 'sa chilla siud, 'sa chille seo, fo
shiantan iarmailt (paisgte, dìon, gus an tig an là)
agus mactalla a dranndail
seachd ciad bliadhna
seachd ciad bliadhna mar cheist

3

bho'n a chuilthionn gu creag ealasaid
bho sgeirean lochlannach
gu crìochan cuimreach
bho'n a pharbh gu maol nan gall
bho ghrunnd na mara gu bàrr nam beann
na tha ann an alba de chlachan
na tha ann an alba de chlachan

4

agus, ars a chomhachag
co chumas cunntas
air an iomadh clach-iùil
eadar alba is saorsa

5

co b'fheàrr leat ars am fitheach
an crois-rathaid, an crois-taghaidh,
cailc, cruaidh, no taise creatha

6

cha b'e cho fada shiubhail i
cha b'ann far an d'fhuair i tàmh,
ro gharbh airson a bhi
na molag am bròg ìmpire
na mùirnean eadar a ruisg,
agus dubh i no geal no liath,

cha b'e a h-anail cheòlar, cha b'è
deàrrsadh sàthach a sùilean
a rinn an tàladh, tha e na gnè
a bhi dall, balbh, is a dà chluas iaruinn,
cha do chùm i riamh
bann-dion air lethsgial,
agus na bha siud de lethsgialan,
thogadh bailten móra leotha,
bailtean móra cloiche
bheireadh fasgadh dion
do shluagh an t-saoghail

7

am faca tusa seo, a choinnich odhair
na do sheann clach fàisneachd
na caoraich lom air achadh lom
agus ballaichean àrd mu'n cuairt orra,
clach teagaimh, clach briaga,
clach eagail, clach aimhreit,
agus aon dòrnag sgàinte dòchais
a ghluaiseas, a dh'fhàgas
toiseach beàrna

The English translation of lia fàil *appeared in the* Scotsman October 1996.

The Weirdstane

1
Did ye hear the walcom cry
an pandemonium forbye,
yon muckle **Stane** cam hame again,
ti ligg lown in its richtfu airt,
as Scotland's langsyne treisure?
For the auld creagh cam back at last –
Did we no gie a cantie blast!

2
Some say it wes the richtfu stane, lang stowed in a cauld bit
atween the flair an royal airse, (sae faur, sae faur awa)
ithers threipt on this kirk, yon kirk, happit frae aa wathers,
hained thare (til the great day comes)
an aye the souch gangs on –
seiven centuars,
seiven centuars,
seiven centuars aye speirin.

Chapman 85

Stoned Alive!

ISBN 0 906772 81 8   ISSN 0308-2695   © *Chapman* 1996

4 Broughton Place, Edinburgh EH1 3RX, Scotland
Tel 0131–557 2207   Fax 0131–556 9565
Editor: Joy Hendry   **Assistant Editor: Sam Wood**
Advertising: Caroline Lindsay   Subscriptions: Margarette Weber
Book Orders: Gerry Stewart
Volunteers: Christina Cree, Sarah Edwards, Joel Kennedy

Submissions:

Chapman welcomes submissions of poetry,
fiction and critical articles provided they are
accompanied by a stamped addressed envelope
or International Reply coupons

Subscriptions:

	Personal		Institutional	
	1 year	2 years	1 year	2 years
UK	£14	£26	£19	£35
Overseas	£19/$32	£35/$59	£23/$39	£42/$69

THE SCOTTISH ARTS COUNCIL

•EDINBVRGH•
THE CITY OF EDINBURGH COUNCIL

Printed by Mayfair Printers, Print House, Commercial Road, Hendon, Sunderland, SR2 8NP.

Editorial

Joy Hendry, the usual writer of *Chapman* editorials, is currently in Austria giving a paper in Salzburg on "How poetry made the nation," and has entrusted the completion of *Chapman* 85 to the Assistant Editor. We hope she enjoyed her time on the Continent as she may well be forced to live out the rest of her days there if I do enough damage to her reputation.

This issue was given the working title *Pick 'n' Mix*. The idea being that it was to be a more eclectic issue than some of our recent volumes which have focused on individual authors. These, while relevant and (I hope) informative, can sometimes seem to be a litany of dead male poets. Hamish Henderson, the last living figure featured, appeared over a year ago (*Chapman* 82); Elspeth Davie, the last woman to grace our covers, in *Chapman* 81. It seemed, then, time to make a break. Even graphic designers were set to work on what we feel is a more up to date cover image.

(Un)fortunately, political events got ahead of us as Michael Forsyth promised the return of what some lovingly call "Scotland's ancestral breeze block". After such news, it seemed necessary to take a look at this phenomenon. To this end, John Ritchie and Robert Brydon try to dispel some of the myths and counter-myths that abound on the subject. Next to this we publish aonghas macneacail's poem "lia fàil" together with a Scots translation by William Neill.

So it seems that we're going from bad to worse and move from dead poets to large lumps of rock. The intended eclecticism survives though with a large amount of Brent Hodgson's poetic fictions; I found Donald S Murray's short story "Gorbachov in Stornoway" so amusing I decided to include another, "Hoover's Housekeeper". Chris Harvie shares thoughts on his travel in Russia and, closer to home, actress Eliza Langland sees the importance of radio to Scottish drama. I could go one, but by now you've seen the contents page. And now ...

A word to our sponsor. *Chapman* has an application pending the SAC's Lottery Department, the results of which we shall know at the end of November. This application is to fund a major upgrade of our office: a new computer and communications system, more powerful database facilities and enable projects like putting *Chapman* on the Web. As you will know, Lottery funding is limited to 75% of the cost of the project and the applicant is expected to show public support by raising the remaining 25%. We are currently having talks with major sponsors, but this, as usual, is difficult, literature not being the most superficially attractive area of the arts to sponsor. We are appealing to you then, our subscribers and readers to give a donation specifically to this Lottery application of any amount you can afford, however small.

You most of all know of our recent achievements: five new collections of poetry published this year (including Janet Paisley whose play, *Refuge*, won the Peggy Ramsay Award); the Chapman National Poetry Tour and events during the Festival at the Grouse House; four more books are due out before the end of the year. The events too continue with a fund-raising celebration of Scots and Gaelic, Tones of Destiny. A star-studded cast will perform under this resonant (!) banner on 28 November at Edinburgh's Assembly Rooms. Further details can be found on the inside front cover.

Sam Wood

3

Frae coolin's pike ti ailsa craig
an frae the norsemans' skerries,
doun ti the cymbric borders
frae cape wrath ti gallowa's mull
frae the sea's grunn til the tapmaist ben
thare's fouth o stanes in Scotland
thare's fouth o stanes in Scotland

4

an wha nou, quo the houlat
sal keep a tallie o
aa the monie lodesman's stanes
atween Scotland an freedom?

5

Whit wad ye, quo the corbie
cross-roads or voter's cross
cauk, steel, or the wat moul?

6

No hou faur it's traivelt
nor whaur it gat ti bide,
faur ower rouch ti be
a cleek on a teirant's shuin,
a jowel atween his brous,
an bleck or white or gray
no its liltin braith, an no
the skyrie glent o'ts een
that beglamourt, it is its wey,
ti bide blinn, deif, an its twa airn lugs,
that wadna haud
a trate on a excaise,
an thare wes nae want o excaises,
haill ceities cud be biggit,
muckle aislar ceities,
that wad tichtlie bield,
the haill fowk o the warld.

7

Did ye see this Kenneth o Brahan
thro yir stane o prophecie?
shorn sheep on a tuim hirst,
heich waas fauldin thaim,
swither-stanes, leein-stanes,
fear-stanes, cangle-stanes
an yin spleet shoddie o howpe
that shifts an shaws
the stairtin o a gap.

Translated from the Gaelic by William Neill.

Shadow of a Dream

John Ritchie and Robert Brydon

The announcement by Michael Forsyth that the Stone of Scone was to be returned to Scotland surprised most people and was hailed by all the newspapers as the return of the Stone of Destiny. It is alarming how ignorant most Scots are about their own history. Hollywood now dictates our history and we Scots believe it. *Braveheart* was a good yarn based on the legend of Wallace, and although most of the story was built round Blind Harry's account of Wallace, it is still for the most part fictional. The same applies for the Stone of Scone as opposed to the Stone of Destiny or the Lia Faill. Indeed, more inaccuracies have grown since the retrieval and the return of the Stone of Scone in early 1950s than existed before. Now Scots are arguing about a stone that Edward I did not want, after all he left it lying unclaimed for five years at Edinburgh castle, and, contrary to present historical statements, he did not take it to London. That can be laid at the door of his son, Edward II.

So at which point in history do we start to tell the story of the two stones? The definitive date has to be summer 1296, the year the true Stone of Destiny was forced into hiding. At this time the duplicity and treachery of the Scottish nobility in the closing decade of the 13th century had plunged the nation into social turmoil. A condition the powerful king of England exploited to his own advantage. The origin of Scotland's regretful state lay in the unexpected death of an infant princess, known to history as 'The Maid of Norway'. Following the death of Alexander III, killed by a fall from his horse at Kinghorn, Margaret had become the sole successor to the throne of Scotland. Even before the death of Alexander, scheming Edward had already entered into negotiations with the King of Norway to arrange a child marriage of convenience between the distant infant Princess and his own six year old son Prince Edward of England. The death of Alexander precipitated matters already afoot in the land, for as the Scots sent a ship for the young successor. Edward pressed ahead with his marriage plan, called the Treaty of Brigham, (18 July 1290) the completion of which would place all Scotland in his grasp, with his son as child king to an infant Queen.

There is a tradition in Scotland that the waters of Treadwells Loch are said to turn red with the death of of one of Scotland's ancient Royal family. On that fateful autumn night in the year 1290, they must have turned blood–red, as the little Princess expired during the rigours of a stormy North sea voyage, and the mournful black-bannered ship entered the port of Leith. In the strife-torn years that followed, many Scottish waters would emulate the colours of Treadwells Loch that night. Within days of the arrival of the ominous ship, no fewer than thirteen noble claimants to the crown of the northern kingdom had come forward, and the land was threatened by vicious civil war. The Lords of Scotland appealed to Edward to arbitrate. He accepted, gilded crown and chain in hand – for the Lion could now adjudicate the Unicorn. He then demanded that on 10 May 1291 the Lords of the North would attend him at his castle at Norham, for the purpose of hearing of the primary claimants, now reduced to eight. The long adjudication began. The Scottish people had desired a king with nothing but Celtic blood and one of undivided loyalty, this was the declared issue of Edward's mandate to arbitrate.

Weeks passed, and the finalists were reduced to the families of Balliol and Bruce. The Scots Lords, now painfully aware of their feet on alien soil and a foreign king deciding the fate of their crown, silently watched the two remaining claimants in turn swear to abide by Edward's decision as their liege and sovereign lord of the land. Edward's favour fell upon his dependent John Balliol. With this choice the Unicorn was finally chained and the die cast for a suicidal war of escape from England's strangling chains. John Balliol was crowned puppet king at Scone on 30 November 1292. Dutifully, Balliol appeared later to do homage to Edward at Newcastle bearing with him the ancient seal of Scotland. Shock, however, attended the faces of the witnesses as Edward took the old and regal seal in his hands, broke it into four pieces and ordered that they be placed in the English treasury as a token of his English dominion.

King Edward's arrogant breaking of the Scottish seal in the face of Balliol, known now as 'Toom Tabard' or 'empty coat,' was literally the ritual act that began those bitter wars of Scottish Independence culminating twenty years later at Bannockburn. Increasing bitterness and frustration with the conquest of Celtic Wales and Scotland produced a gnawing malice in the now ageing King. Edward introduced the cruel slow torture of hanging drawing and quartering, a personal invention so that he might watch his captive Welsh nobles die. He also applied this same fate to terrified Scots, whilst occupying himself with the prophecies of Merlin, the legends of Arthur, and letters to the Pope claiming descent from the ancient kings of Troy.

As his megalomania grew, so evidently did Edward's desire to possess the Stone of Destiny. The mediaeval chronicle *De Mellsa* records a legend existing in Edward's lifetime thus: "After declaring that the Scots brought the Stone from Egypt, by reason that Moses prophesied, a Prince would sit upon that throne who would rule over many islands". Biblical legend tells us that the Stone of Destiny is said to have been the stone which Jacob used as a pillow at Bethel, where he had a dream or vision of the ladder to heaven. It is said that when he awoke Jacob rose up in the morning and took the stone that had been his pillow, set it up as a pillar and poured oil on it and vowed "this stone that I set as a pillow, shall be God's house, and all that thou shalt give me I will surely give a tenth unto Thee". The message that Jacob was said to have been given, was that his seed would spread to the four corners of the world, and when this was achieved then his seed would return to this land and it would be called Israel. Through all this time God promised to be with Jacob's successors until the prophecy was fulfilled.

The present Coronation Stone is a roughly rectangular hewn block of coarse-grained, reddish-grey sandstone, and is 673 x 419 x 279 mm (26.5" x 16.5" x 11"). It lies in a boxlike space under the seat of the Coronation Chair. According to legend, the Stone of Destiny was in existence long before the birth of Christ. The true history of the Stone of Scone or the present Coronation Stone, however, is only traceable from the thirteenth century onwards. The Scottish chronicler John de Fordun, has left us a lengthy account of the coronation of Alexander III of Scotland upon the stone at Scone in the year 1249. Rishanger, another chronicler of the early fourteenth century, who was present, also records the use of the stone in the coronation of John Balliol. Walter de Hemingford, Edward the First's chronicler, was also present at Balliol's coronation. Hardyng and other early historians of Scotland describe at length how Edward I, after he had overrun Scotland in 1296 removed a stone from Scone.

Further, among the king's jewels which were in the Edinburgh Castle in 1296 is described *"una petra magna super quam Reges Scotiae solebant coronari;"* and in the wardrobe accounts of Edward I for 1300 there is a payment to Magistro Waltero Pictori, for the construction of the present Coronation Chair to contain the Stone of Scone.

This stone has been examined by successive generations of geologists. Many scientists have examined microscope sections of sand-grains and of a small porphyrite pebble obtained from the stone by Sir Jethro Teall while it was being cleaned 1892. The abundant grains of quartz, scarce alkali-feldspar, muscovite and decomposed biotite have been compared with similar rocks from various geological horizons, and the Coronation Stone is seen to agree most closely with sandstones of Lower Old Red Sandstone age from Scotland. Such rocks are well developed in the neighbourhood of Scone and Dundee. Specimens obtained from these areas frequently carry pebbles of porphyrite or andesite, some of which are petrographically identical with the one from the Coronation Stone. One or two similar pebbles, about the size of a pea, may be seen in the Stone of Westminster.

A widespread belief exists that the 'Stone of Destiny' was once kept at Dunstaffnage in Argyll, and removed from there to Scone by Kenneth MacAlpin in 843. John Macculloch, however, in his pioneer geological work, *A Description of the Western Islands of Scotland* (1819), notes that the Coronation Stone is a calcareous sandstone exactly resembling that forming the doorway of Dunstaffanage Castle. But from a recent examination it is evident that the sandstones forming the voussoirs of its doorway are not Old Red Sandstone similar to the Coronation Stone, but are of Triassic age, probably from Carsaig, in Mull – a locality which appears also to have supplied the rock employed in parts of Iona Cathedral, the Rodel Kirk in South Harris, and probably other Hebridean buildings of mediaeval date. The coarse Old Red Sandstone conglomerate on which Dunstaffnage Castle stands is quite dissimilar from the Stone of Scone, and there is no evidence for the stone having originated from this area. The balance of evidence, therefore, is in favour of the stone having been quarried somewhere in the east of Perthshire or in southern Angus, probably not far from the ancient seat of the Pictish monarchy at Scone.

The earliest mention of Scone was in 710 AD when it was the Pictish capital which it continued to be up to 843 AD when it was amalgamated with the Scots Kingdom by Kenneth MacAlpin after the last great battle between the Picts and the Scots. It was Kenneth who brought the *Lia Faill* or Stone of Destiny to Scone. The Abbey of Scone was founded in 1115, but had been an important ecclesiastical centre many centuries prior to this date, receiving its royal charter in 906.

The ancient council of Scotland was held at Moothill in Scone. Moothill was also where Nectan III the Pictish King dedicated his church to the Holy Trinity, the official marriage of the Culdean and the Roman church. From this union the mound received the name the Hill of Belief. Moothill, the mound or hill (an area of 100yds by 60yds) is said to have been created by the custom of the lords, barons and landowners bringing to a coronation, a bootfull of earth from each area of Scotland that they represented. This meant that the King was crowned on all the soil of Scotland, thus ensuring his ancient custodial right. Malcolm I, who gave all his land to his nobles after they won him a great battle against the Vikings, further emphasised the importance of Moothill by stating that it was the only land he owned; thus by owning Moothill he was the caretaker of all of Scotland.

The Scottish people, and in particular, the Scottish church were fervently aware of the importance of the Stone of Destiny remaining in Scotland. It was the nation's most important talisman, the sacred embodiment of the privilege of the Scots to crown their own King. Its history in Scotland originated with Fergus I who brought it from Tara in Ireland. As is well known, the Stone of Destiny has an immense legendary history which identifies it with Jacob's Pillow, the sacred stone of Ireland, and that Chair of St. Columba which was always referred to as the Marble Chair. It can be said with certainty, however, that the stone in Westminster was regarded as a sacred one only as far back as the fourteenth century. At some period a rectangular sinking has been marked out in the middle of the top surface, where there is also a roughly cut Latin cross. On each side of the stone are iron rings said to be so placed to enable a pole to be passed through them for the purpose of carrying the stone. However when a stone of this weight is carried in such a way it begins to pendulate and cannot be carried any distance, the only possible use for the rings would be to aid lifting. To find any true description of the Stone of Destiny, we must look at the great seals of the Scottish Kings prior to Bruce. There is an illustration in the letter D of David in the Kelso charter showing the king sitting on a round stone. Other the seals show the kings, including John Balliol, sitting on a round polished stone. We must also look at Hemingford's account of John Balliol's coronation with the stone described thus: "*Concavus, Quidem ad Modem Rotundae Cathedrae Confectus*". This description concurs with Adam de Rishanger, and John de Fordun's description of Alexander III's coronation. All these chronicles state that the coronation stone was a black, round, polished stone; shaped like a chair with inscriptions.

The Stone's hiding place had always been a secret known to a few trusted people. The only time it was ever seen in public was at a coronation and then only at a distance. After the coronation it would be returned to its sanctuary. Not more than a handful of people would have been privy to the place of concealment; people who would have given up their lives rather than reveal its secret resting place.

King Edward desired to eradicate anything which represented or preserved the patriotic independence of the country he had invaded. Historians affirm that in its progress through Scotland, Edward's army under direct orders sought out and destroyed every monument connected with the antiquity of the nation. Peculiarly Edward ordered his soldiers back to Scone and instructed them to pull the abbey apart. This was two years after the 'stone' is recorded as "on deposit" at Edinburgh Castle. Edward was said to have almost destroyed Scone trying to discover some object's location. He had his soldiers level several buildings to pressurise the residents into revealing the hiding place of Scotland's palladium. We are told that these men were particularly brutal, killing and torturing in their quest. The Abbot of Scone was said to be so disturbed by the behaviour of the soldiers that he complained to Edward. Edward retorted that they would continue this treatment until the hidden object was found. With this in mind, whilst at Scone he had the ancient chartulary of the abbey demolished as this was the premiere depository of Scotland's ancient history with historical notices and charters, which would have contained knowledge fatal to his pretended claim of superiority. Seals and charters of the abbey were also destroyed.

Hemingford tells us: "At the monastery of Scone was placed a large stone in the church of God, near the great altar, hollowed out like a round chair, in which future Kings of Scots were placed, according to custom, as the place of their coronation". This would appear to be the same description he gave of John Balliol's coronation. The statement that has always been reported, would appear to have been added later: "Returning by Scone, the king ordered the stone on which the Kings of Scotland were wont to be placed at their coronation be taken to London as a sign that the kingdom had been conquered and resigned".

The second part of this report would suggest that Hemingford was not present at Scone and was merely reporting on Edward's issued order, for the stone taken by Edward's soldiers bears no resemblance to Hemingford's earlier description. Did the disheartened Abbot of Scone decided to give the soldiers a stone from the altar of one of the ruined church buildings? A stone already dressed with an iron ring on each end? Swearing to the commander of the soldiers that this was the sacred stone? Edward of course would have been aware of what the real Stone looked like. He would have questioned both Rishanger and Hemingford and was also familiar with the Royal seals. Edward evidently did not have what he was looking for. Instead of a triumphant procession down to London, we find the wardrobe master at Edinburgh Castle writing to Edward in 1301 asking what he wants done with the '*Petra Magnum*' or 'Great Stone' in his care.

Another piece of evidence is that Edward had ordered Magistro Waltero Pictori to create a magnificent bronze throne to be made to contain Scotland's Stone of Destiny. The present wooden throne was created as a casting pattern for the bronze throne. By 1300, when Walter was finally paid £5.00 for the work, Edward's enthusiasm for the magnificent bronze throne waned. Why? The stone from Scone still lay at Edinburgh castle. Why? As we have stated earlier Edward was well acquainted with Hemingford's chronicle, so he was well aware that the '*Petra Magnum*' was not the Stone of Destiny. However not many people were party to this information. It is possible that Edward pulled off one of the great con-tricks of history. Robert the Bruce was crowned in a ceremony at Scone on 25 March 1306, in which it is recorded that the Abbot of Scone, hereditary keeper of the "Fatal Chair", produced a "chair" for this Coronation. Many years later, the Treaty of Edinburgh (17 March 1328), between Robert the Bruce and Edward III, ratified later that year as the Treaty of Northampton, recognised the sovereignty of Scotland as an Independent Nation. The English therein offered to return the Stone from Westminster. The Scots politely declined their offer, asking for the Holy Rood of St. Margaret instead.

Perhaps the Westminster Stone is being returned to us because Robbie the Pict raised sufficient funds and wrote enough letters to worry the government into returning the Stone. That same government that takes its lineage from Edward's Model Parliament of 1295*, created to raise money for the invasion of Scotland. Frankly a piece of Perthshire sandstone that certainly has more to do with the coronations of English Kings and Queens from Edward II to the present monarch than it ever it ever had with the early lineage of the Scottish Crown is being returned to Scotland. But, perhaps this Stone symbolises the chip that the Scots have always had on their shoulder about the English, or vice versa!.

As to the Stone of Destiny, the true *Lia Faill*. The prophecy stands, that it will not appear until Scotland is a separate and independent nation and reaffirms its own Destiny.

* Model Parliament: English parliament set up 1295 by Edward I; it was the first to include representatives from outside the clergy and aristocracy, and was established because Edward needed the support of the whole country against his opponents: Wales, France, and Scotland. His sole aim was to raise money for military purposes, and the parliament did not pass any legislation. The parliament comprised archbishops, bishops, abbots, earls, and barons (all summoned by special writ, and later forming the basis of the House of Lords); also present were the lower clergy (heads of chapters, archdeacons, two clerics from each diocese, and one from each cathedral) and representatives of the shires, cities, and boroughs (two knights from every shire, two representatives from each city, and two burghers from each borough).

Yer Man's Story

John Hamilton

"What wid ye think," said yer man, pausing to sook the Guinnesss off his moustache, "o a bunch o people who borrowed somethin, never got roun tae giein it back, lost it, well not exactly lost it, they knew where it was, but they did bugger all about gettin it back. And then when they were offered it back sat aroun arguin as tae which wan o them had the right and proper place tae keep it. Entirely slipped their minds that they only had a loan o it in the furst place. Bunch o arseholes wid ye say?" He took a long draw on his pint.

"Talk aboot ripples from a stane, two thousand years and the ripples are runnin yet . . . washin through yer bloody medja here and bloody now.

Ye see, afore things was written down, afore the Celts, the Islands o Ireland was a busy enough place. Them in charge was the De Danaan, most o the place, not Connaught, but that's anither story. When the first boatloads o Celts arrived there wis a few skirmishes, aye, when is there no a few skirmishes. Anyway, wan thing aboot the Celts, the main thing aboot the Celts, is that ye dinnae fuck aboot wi the Celts – not if ye value the attachment o yer heid tae yer body. And the De Danaan werenae dim.

So they split. Buggered off tae what Captain Kirk wid cry a parallel universe. Steyed where they were, same place, same landscape but invisible to the human mortals. Damn good trick if ye can get the knack o it. And they're there tae this day. Course there's sparks fly when wan world knocks against the ither Happens aa the time – some o them slippin through tae here, humans taken there. Aa this crack aboot Spaceships? I dinnae ken, you lot hae nae imagination at aa.

No every day, ye ken, people goin back an forth. Often enough. Sort o thing disnae get written doon. But look at the stories, they're fu o it. The Fairy Kingdom – Fair Elfland – Bollocks! Ye'd sooner mak oot it's kids stuff than uise yer bloody imagination. At least Captain Kirk kent an Alternative Universe when it came up an kicked him in the arse. Tuatha De Danaan, grandchildren of Dana – wan chorus o 'All Kinds of Everything' an Ah'll box yer bloody ears. Long memories. Wild long. Comes fae livin for ever. Live forever unless some bloody Celt wheechs their heids aff.

Thing is where did the De Danaan come frae? The West. From oot o the settin sun. Ay, there's much ye cannae see. The land o the Deid. Also known as the Land o the Livin. Yes, it is an Irish Story. See, "after death" was a dacent sort o place, light an pleasure, no fire an brimstone. Heaven, if ye like. The De Danaan came frae Heaven. An they brought four things, wan frae each o the four cities o Heaven. A Magic Sword and a Magic Spear, naturally. Nae dacent battle wis ever fought in the stories withoot at least someb'dy haein a magic weapon o some sort. An a pot.

The Cauldron o the Dagda wis a pot ye could cook in, feed an army and it wad never be emp'y. Ma Mither had wan like that. Whit did they cook? Irish Stew o course. D'ye ken I've heard people arguin aboot the right and proper recipe fur Irish Stew. Well, I'll have you know ma Mither's as Irish as ony stane on the Giant's Causeway, an when she makes a stew, that's Irish Stew – right an proper. Man, that gravy, ye ken when the spuds have collapsed and dissolved and ye're right doon intae the magic at the bottom o the pot. Ye ken? Ach, ye dinnae ken, ye heathen." He was lost in reverie for some time. He licked his lips and took another swallow of Guinness.

"Tae get tae the point. Ay there is a bloody point. Where wis I? O ay, the fourth thing, frae the City of Falias, wis the Lia Fall. An whenever they skipped oot o the mortal world, the Lia Fall wis left behind. At Tara. Place o the High Kings. It became part o the King's possessions, handed down. For Centuries. Until . . ." He sat upright and began stabbing at the table with an aggressive forefinger.

"Until the Sixth Century Anno Fuckin' Domino, when wan Fergus, son of Erc, cried hissel Fergus the Great, wis aboot tae be crowned king . . . *Of Scotland.* He asked his brother, Murtagh, by coincidence also a son of Erc, who happened tae be the High King o Ireland at the time, if ye could borrow, note *borrow* the Lia Fail fur his coronation. Well, Murtagh wis a dacent sort o chap, so he sent it over and it never went back. The rest is history, written doon stuff. Youse buggers had it for six centuries then let some English Arsehole pinch it.

Ay, translate it, man, Lia Fail – Stane o Destiny. So if ye should happen tae hear onybody arguin aboot its right an proper place, ye could remind them that it came from Ireland, and it cam tae Ireland straight oot o heaven. This is a serious piece o masonry."

He rose unsteadily, drained his pint, pointed straight at me, "And don't you forget it! Arseholes!" he said, and staggered in the direction of the bar.

John Hamilton

Wee Magic Stane (Variation)

No, wan king o England, when North on a spree,
Wis helpin himsel tae whitever he'd see,
Thocht tae himsel he could maybe find room,
Under his seat for a big stane frae Scone.

Noo this King, wan Edward, wis not a nice lot,
His hobby he'd aye gie as hammerin Scots.
His pals took the stane jist as if it wis theirs
An keepit it parked in ablo the King's erse.

On the day o the Union, the fact wis confirmed,
Nae way the stane wad noo be returned,
Fur them doon in London, they aye took the line,
"Whit's yours is noo oors, whit's mines is still mines!"

Till a couple o lads made a plan fur the crack,
Tae gang doon tae London tae win the stane back,
Crept intae Westminster an oot the back gate
Wi a big lump of stane for tae repatriate.

When them at Westminster keeked under the throne,
Some Scotch rotters pilfered our Destiny Stone,
To take what was theirs well it's all a bit much."
And they muttered sae derkly aboot Treason and such.

Well they quarried a stane o a similar stuff
An dressed it all up till it looked good enough.
They caa'd in the press an announced that the stane,
Had been found an returned tae Westminster again.

When the reivers fund oot whit Westminster had done,
They went aroond diggin up stanes by the ton,
When each wis completed they issued the claim
That this wis the true an original stane.

But the cream o the joke, well it's still tae be tellt,
Fur the lad that wis runnin them aff on the belt
At the peak o production wis so sorely pressed
That the real yin got bunged in alang wi the rest.

So if ye should come on a stane wi a ring
Jist sit yersel doon an proclaim yersel King,
Fur there's naebody oot there that can challenge yer claim
That you were crooned King on the Destiny Stane.

Sae listen John Major, ye must think we're all daft,
Tae gie us a stane and tae hae the last laugh,
But the power in the stane well it's no feenished yet
And this flippant gesture ye'll live tae regret.

Brent Hodgson

God Vesetes the Lond of the Scots

Ane day God the Kyng of Hevene seide te Seinte Peter:
"Halden the fort for a litel while Pete,
I departe te the eorthe te vesete the Lond of the Scots."

And Seinte Peter seide:
"Wulle you clethe tham Scots that ere clatheles?
Gyffe drynke te tham that ere thristy?
Helpe tham that lyes in presoun?
Gyffe herber te tham that ere housles?
Fede tham that ere hunngry?"

God herd thise words of the seinte and he onswerede:
"Ya, ther es a nede for that - thay hafe a Tory government.
And whon I beon in that lond undur hevene,
I schal make the sonne ful brihte appon that lond."

Seinte Peter bad foure angelus te gan with God and soone thay wente forthe,
And thay coomen te the cete of Paryce wher ane angel, his nome wes Fred,
Wenten togedere with a wommon. The othur thre angelus seide te God:
"We hafe gret envye of Fredes joye and of his blisse,
Can we slepe with thise wymmen that weore iboren in Paryce?"
And God asket:
"Whuch of you seke the delit of the companye of realle wymmen?"
The thre angelus gaf this onswere:
"We alle do."

And God Almihti spac thise words:
"It es a wundurfol ighe, luve,"
Tellen the thre angelus te gan anon.
The firste angel Dauvit bleugh the spirit of lyf inte the swete mought of Marie.
The secunde angel Johne bicluppet the lusti bodi of Cecille.
The thirde angel Sandy he wolde lygge with a gredy wommon,
Hire nome wes Gloria, G-L-O-R-I-A, Gloria.

God he passeth te the Lond of the Scots and the folk that dwellet ther,
Bathe yung and eldre, weore weopen:
The aer wes kalde;
The wynds thay weoren not pesible;
The snouh wes thikke on the grounde;
The beestes of the feelde dude couchen in muk.

God he sendeth doun the fuir of the sonne:
And he maad the watur te schine as brihte as the sonnebeem,
And he maad the se calme and softe the weders of the aer,

And he maad the flurs fayr and ferme:
And he maad the gras as grene as eni gras!
And he maad beestes of alle manere beo of goode herte;
And he maad houses and festes and songs withouten ende;
And he maad the sonne ful brihte withouten cese appon the lond.

Forty weeks passeth and God wes in his heghe offyce,
Whon the clerkes of the Haly Kyrke spac te him:
"Men schulde seo Goddes werkes,
Bote aboute this we hafe a grucche;
The sonne schineth daye aftur daye over the Lond of the Scots.
Ther es mete and drynk in plente.
Men and wymmen ere going clatheles and bathe ere hoppin:
The wymmen scheawe the burtherne of their breostes,
Wymmen and men scheawe their membris be daye and nighte;
Lorde, ther es al manere of venyal synn.
Kyng of Hevene we beseche thee, enden your werkes.
Make the Scots housles to wander in the storme,
Make tham suffre, make tham perische in the kalde,
Make the men geten peynes of helle in bodi and sawl ones ageyn.
Make the wymmen thole the custome of wysshen disches ones ageyn.
Make the weddid and the sengle wymmen gedren messages ones
ageyn."

God on heghe herde the biddyng of the clerkes of the Haly Kryke:
And he maad the sonne ful brithe appon the Lond of the Scots for
evermore. ENDE.

herber - shelter; iboren - born; cete of Paryce - the city of Paris; ighe -
eye; bicluppet - embraced; gredy - eager; pesible - peaceful; couchen -
lie; lusti - beautiful; grucche - grudge; hoppin - jumping with joy;
membris - genitals; gedren - gather, collect;

Ane Essay on Chucken Soop

Chucken Soop is a gude friend of mine but what is Chucken Soop?
Any combination of Watur and the Futesteps of a Chucken
Is theoretically Chucken Soop,
For example, a Pan of Watur through whuch a Chucken has walked.

Who invented Chucken Soop?
The Romans invented Chucken Soop.
On the seven hills of Rome the Romans carried out animal sacrifices,
And the Watur through whuch a Chucken had walked
Would run down into the River Tiber,
Making it a perfect spot for the Canning of Chucken Soop.

Has anyone famust ever eaten Chucken Soop?
Yes, the Courtiers of Quene Elizabeth 1 proudly clamed that sche -
"Hath a Bowl of Chucken Soop everie Thrie Minutes,

Whether sche nedeth hit or not."

Whon did Chucken Soop become universally popular?
It become popular with the Public at large
After the Advent of the Eight to Late Spar Supermarket chain.

Do I eat Chucken Soop?
Yes, I am a moderate consumer;
Last yeir I ate forty-sevin thusent cans of Chucken Soop.

Born In A Pallace

. . . Grandfather was a big man, his constant companion
was Ben a boxer dog. Ben used to jam a fat cigar
between his jaws. He was sociable by nature
and Ben often entertained American visitors.

On the whole my father opposed change,
be believed in the old traditions.
Mr Sprogg, a Scotsman, administered the pallace.
There was no running water in his quarters.

After my grandfather died, I sat in his green leather chair.

Despite the immense size of the pallace, with its secret staircases,
- blue wallpaper in my bedroom, I spent most of my life in Florence,
which was like a fifth home to me.
I showed my friends around Florence for days on end,
and still found time to dress up.

Florence was a city full, of design ideas.

A Russian Nobilman Vesetes A Gorbals Grocer.

"I have heard it was the suster of Lassie who reskewed me
From the river yonder. I have heard that Lassie has saved the world
On more than one momentous occasion.
There I was drowning in the waters of the Clyde,
- Reeking of rich leather perfume,
When that dog unexpectedly stayed me from extinction."

"Shopkeeper! I wish to buy an oliphant.
And tell me, how should he be ridden?"

"Sold out!
What sort of corner shop is this?
Maxim Gorky! I must look a fule.
Shopkeeper, I am Count Orlov; let us do a swop.
Ten peasants shall be yours and Lassie's suster shall be mine.
A dog who has reskewed a Russian nobilman
Will make a fortune in Holyrood."

"Eh? Hollywood?"
"Aye, Lassie's suster will make a fortune in Hollywood."

"Jesus Crist! What do you mean?
That dog does not belong to you ..."

Cherry the Film Star Mouse.

Cherry survived a troubled mousehood in Edinburgh:
Hir fader and moder spent all their tyme in a laboratory.

Just before hir third birthday sche sailed for the U.S.,
And stayed in a shoe cupboard at the Plaza, New York.
Sche was discovered as "Mouse of the Yeir"
When nestling in a pair of high heels by Long Tail Silver,
The Hollywood film director; he was short and square
But he had good manners.

Stripped off nakit for hir debut in "Wildlife Special"
- "It was my chance to become a film star,
And I did not want to say no."

Subsequently starred in many films with Muckey Mouse,
With whom sche had sexy scenes, and played
The leading role in "Shag Fred Dead".

Hir career suffered a setback when sche became addicted
To strawberry-flavoured milk, Rocquefort cheese,
And the powdered nibs of the xocolate tree.
Cherry decided to brave the scandal,
And signed a contract with a respectable American publisher,
Receiving an advance payment of £ 450,000 -
To write the story of hir lyfe.

I Am A Female Budgie

There is one budgie in my life and his name is Herbert.
Beware of Rhode Island Reds he said to me one day.
I asked why?
Because they are chickens he said.
I am not a road sweeper: I am a freedom-loving budgie,
I got married before I was fully fledged.
Someone wrote a letter to the Quene about me and Herbert.
She said the laws governing the conduct of budgies are under review.
The Houses of Parliament blew up yesterday.
A policeman came to question me:
Had I seen a dark budgie go by,
Carrying a home-made bomb?
Be careful how you reply,
Herbert said to me.

Jenni Daiches

Pacific city

Salt seasons the tang
of eucalyptus. In the lucent
bay the dark water
is where the currents race.

A man as black as deep sea
sits by the road with a pair
of orange cats curled on his lap,
littoral, crowds breaking at his feet.

I step in and out
of new worlds bewitched
by incongruity.
The sun burns through sea fog.

Runners pass obliquely
on the shore where missions unfolded,
where wagons from the mountains
raised pillars of dust.

Gold was trapped in the rivers.
Banks were built to hold back earthquakes.
Ships flexed their sails
at the ocean's chasmic gate.

Now they mix cocktails
where they canned sardines.
Black hands have riveted,
swung hammers, hefted bricks.

They bind the orange fur.
The ocean a blue but forbidden
passage, the green mountains
a magnificent illusion.

Endgame

Norse-carved 12th-century chessmen were found in 1831 on a beach at Uig on the island of Lewis and sold to National Museums of Scotland.

What battles on a blue shore
scarred your rocky face?
Smile, King.
Those days are gone.
You're muffled now in centuries
misty as mountains,
soft as rain.

You were born in the sea.
Sired by a walrus,
licked clean by spindrift,
nursed by an artist whose name
has vanished.
Open your mouth, Queen.
Sing to me.

Bishop, you poured words
like milk, a little warmth
against the cold of wind and sword,
the shiver of hunger.
Yet your eyes
are all silence.

Your body's as hard
as helmet and shield,
your anger cold. Knight,
do you rage because you've played
your last game in the sand,
and a hollow resounds
where your ivory relics were found?

Your fortress is held
in the palm of a hand.
Make your move, Castle, prove
that all was not lost
on the blue shore where your people
fought with time
and burial shrouded your walls.

It's been a long
captivity. Pawn, you are small
and might slip easily
through enemy lines, the lights
and the sentinels. Listen.
The sea. The dip of oars,
the smack of wind in the sails.
Rouse your people. Free them
from the soft, insidious years,
return to the blue shore.

Demolition

The wind inside the stone,
the throb of roof and wall,
my attic room inhales the elements,
acts out earthquake.

This morning's news ablaze
with thousands dead in Kobe.
A bomb could have dropped, but it's only
the grinding of earth.

As if nature yearns to destroy.
My walk to work passes
the corner site where demolition's
down to the last raw bricks.
Men taking a building apart,
as if humanity has no choice,
as if nature demands we submit.

Insomnia

Heat blankets this room
and my sleepless body is clothed
in a second skin of sweat.
The air is too heavy for sound
except for the dense tremor
of the train achieving the bridge,
and, oddly, a sea bird
crying in the night.

The stillness so intense
the throb of steel wells
from the cavity of limbs
and the bird mourns as if locked
in the beat of my heart.

In a corner hovers sleep.
At the margins of the bed
the day's abrasions
repel the comforts of the dark.
Another train like hooves
muffled by fog, a hot,
arrested thunder in my head.

James Deahl

The Loneliness of Stones

The sun rises distant and aloof.
People come and go
seeming to enter or leave the room.
All day the table stands in bright sunlight
holding a bowl of fruit.

The business of life occurs.
Tobacco, coffee,
Rachmaninoff's *Symphony in E Minor*
tempt the heart from its cage of flesh.
Children are born in the darkness
between their mothers' legs.

And we are all born
from the cry of skin touching,
from that burning,
impossible hunger.

In the evening I consider
the loneliness of stones:
how they come from deep under the earth
only to return
to their primal fire.

A window opens and closes.
The night's last bell strikes home,
its sound entering the black doorways.

Prelude to Departure

Already summer is fading;
the final day-lilies twist and fall.
I wait patiently for goldenrod,
forever in its coming.

'96   The loneliness of Staves.

As always, I note
the passage of time,
life's daily brutalities,
the sudden possibility of death.

At midnight I feel the stars move
as their light towers above me.
I open wide,
strain into their blackness.

And the blackness comes.
In the cold hour it enters my pupil,
wells up like the dark canto
of workmen from beyond the tide.

Prayer for the Dead in September

All evening that bird
has called from his weeping beech,

now the Pleiades pierce the heart of Heaven,
welcome the pain of the first iron frost.

In flowing robes the sisters turn and
return across this harvest earth.

And the dead, so still in their lying down,
seem truly beyond words -

yet words ascend the transfiguring dark.
There are no good-byes,

only a scattering of prayer candles
and the thin grass awaiting

winter's Grace.

Los Alamos

Le feu jamais ne guérira de nous,
Le feu qui parle notre langue.

- Jacques Dupin

They journey
deeper into the desert,
into that arid juncture
of sun and the dry west wind.

Land of adobe and dust,
of canyons under burning skies.
Every rock wall holds a face,
a memory of events past.

It is not the heat
nor the lack of water
that will kill, but
the expectations of pleasure

forever unfulfilled.
The men advance,
become dust devils
beating on blind stone;

become those who will speak
into the mineral dark
words that may someday
destroy our world.

Pittsburgh X

Below Westinghouse Bridge stretched the plant where
Uncle George acquired great wealth and father
earned his keep. On Family Days his lightning
snapped from Van de Graaff machines to light the
vast and sullied dream. Thousands worked along
Turtle Creek, their generating station
banishing turtles and all else with heat.

Still every spring until the end was near
that creek snarled through East Pittsburgh grey with rage
tearing sandbags from blind factory doors.
Once I watched it swirl ten feet deep; parked cars
packed tight with slime. Now gutted buildings slump
beside cold waters filled again with life.

If Only

our lives could stay
at high autumn,
our bodies entwined
throughout the long
cool night.

If only these haws
could remain on their trees,
red lanterns
lighting our path
through early dusk.

The Trainee Accountant's Fantasy

Gary Egan

Alistair Tick was on his way back to the office after lunch when the chain on his bike came off again. He swore, jumped off and overturned the bike so that it rested on handlebars and saddle. After two minutes' tinkering he succeeded in reinstating the chain. His hands were smeared with oil by now. He was just about to fish a tissue out of his jacket-pocket when a tall woman walked up to him and smiled...

"Having trouble? Let me help." Her hand reached inside his pocket and started to rummage.

"Really," began Alistair, reddening, "there's no need –"

"It's not in that pocket," the woman declared. "Not unless it's caught up in your plastic artillery division."

"My what?" gaped Alistair.

"Your cashcards and ID and what-have-you – all the artillery essential to the post-Hiroshima commuter. Or so they say. Mind you, they'll say anything."

Having shuffled his plastic artillery division like a croupier, she returned it to his pocket. Before he could protest her hand was inside his other pocket. Passers-by stared, but the rummaging woman persisted. Not a bother on her.

"Actually I just remembered I used up my last tissue –"

"Then you must take one of mine." She produced one instantly.

"Thank you." Alistair wiped his hands, studying the woman's features furtively. They were by no means plain but not nearly as striking as her manner, which he considered extraordinary.

"Now shake," commanded the woman. "You can call me Lucasta."

"I'm Alistair – Alistair Tick," mumbled Alistair.

"Who'd credit it?" She tilted her head to one side quizzically. "You don't look like a chartered accountant...But I bet all the girls tell you that."

"I'm only a trainee, as a matter of fact. I –"

"So long, Al," she cut him short, "I must dash. I'll be seeing you. Here, give me that."

She took the used tissue, dropped it in the bin, pressed another into his hand, then sauntered off down the High Street. When she didn't stop at the traffic lights but walked straight on, Alistair wasn't surprised. She had that right of way about her. He set his bike upright again and mounted it uncertainly. He wobbled left into the street where the offices of Hanson, Ferguson & Macauley were situated. Not feeling like a chartered accountant.

Alistair locked his bike in the garage adjacent to the apartments where he lived. It had been a distracting afternoon. The other trainees had ragged him mercilessly about his taste in indelible hand-oils and, after the encounter with Lucasta, balance-sheets had lost the their power to seduce his undivided attention. Eros had begun to creep into his calculations.

Lucasta had aroused his misgivings about accounting as a career. Before he even woke up two decisions had already been made for him: what time he woke up and what he should wear. He felt old – a round-shouldered accountant in a square hole. He dreaded becoming one of those who found crawling so rewarding they forgot how to walk upright, taking files to bed and emerging with in-growing portmanteaux. Even when they weren't crawling they spent so much of their lives on tiptoe they had practically evolved into a new digitigrade species.

Suddenly a terrific downpour ensued, precipitating Alistair's 100-yard sprint to the back garden to salvage his sheets from the clothes-line. He couldn't fail to notice the black panties and suspenders on either side of the sheets. Too risqué for his landlady, they must either belong to his landlady's niece or else one of Roland's girlfriends, deduced Alistair. Roland was the tenant who lived across the hall from him.

He glanced back at the house, but saw nobody rushing to retrieve them. He hesitated, then unpegged them, bundling them up inside his sheets.

As he was climbing the stair, the door of Roland's apartment opened and Lucasta stepped out. Alistair was so astonished he almost dropped the bundle of sheets.

"You!" he cried.

"Yes," agreed Lucasta, still smiling. "Fancy meeting you here."

"I live here," Alistair explained superfluously.

"Really?" But she didn't really sound surprised. "Is it raining very heavily?"

"Well, it's only just started, but it's lashing, yes."

"I'd better get out of my slippers and into my skates, then, hadn't I?"

"Oh," Alistair blushed, "were those things on the line yours?"

"The skimpies, yes."

"That's alright, then. I have them here." He added lamely, "I didn't like to see them get wet."

Lucasta beamed and squeezed his arm.

"I'm touched, Alistair. That was very neighbourly of you. A less considerate tenant would have let them soak. Come in, I'll make you a mug of cocoa."

Before he could refuse, she turned and disappeared back into Roland's apartment. He followed her in.

"Dump those on the sofa and make yourself at home," Lucasta called to him over her shoulder.

Alistair glanced around the apartment. Despite the compelling presence of a black bin-liner bursting with female clothes, everything about the place suggested a male adolescent's "pad". Guitars hooked up to amplifiers. Rugby trophies across the mantelpiece. Calendar girls on the wall –

Lucasta returned with two mugs of cocoa.

"Here, I'll take your jacket. You must be drenched."

It was hardly wet at all, but since Lucasta seemed set on having it Alistair didn't like to disoblige.

"Have you just moved in?" he asked - again, somewhat superfluously. There was something about Lucasta that made most conversation seem superfluous.

"A couple of hours before you got back. By the way, where did you stash my skimpies?"

"Er, they're still between the sheets. Shall I separate them?"

"Not yet. We're only just getting to know each other." She sipped her cocoa and stared at him shamelessly. "Tell me, would you have done the same for Roland's underwear?"

Alistair blushed, more forcefully this time.

"Well...No, probably not ... I don't think I would have, no."

Lucasta allowed a pause during which Alistair's blushes could subside, then inquired: "How's your chain since?"

"Fine," laughed Alistair. "I won't say there hasn't been a squeak out of it – it's still making funny noises – but at least it hasn't come off on me again."

"I'm no good with chains, either."

"You don't like being tied down, I suppose. That's understandable."

Lucasta smiled that smile again.

"Not every night, but I'll try anything once."

Alistair looked away, but walked straight into a calendar girl. Lucasta continued, unruffled: "I'd say Roland'd be able to fix it, no problem. He's good with his hands. Or so he likes to think. When it comes to machines, maybe, but I can't see him bringing in lingerie off the line somehow."

"Have you known Roland long?" Alistair felt he had to say something, fast.

"Not as long as I've known you."

"He'll need a van to move his stuff, I suppose," hinted Alistair, indicating Roland's possessions with what he meant to be a vague sweep of the hand, but once again succeeded unerringly in locating the calendar-girls.

"I suppose he would, yes."

Lucasta was staring at him expectantly. Fascinated and unnerved at the same time, Alistair rose. "Time I was getting along...thanks a million for the cocoa, Lucasta. I'm delighted to see you for a neighbour and I look forward to having you –" He stopped, improvising clumsily –"...round sometime in the near future."

"You bet."

"And we're bound to run into one another on the stair from time to time," struggled Alistair. Lucasta's eyes were making his leave-taking exceptionally difficult.

"You can bank on it," confirmed Lucasta, but the look in her eye did not suggest a strict Catholic upbringing. "I'll get your coat."

She excavated his jacket from the pile where she had unceremoniously dumped it.

"Arms out."

Alistair obeyed. Lucasta slipped the jacket over his shoulders, spun him round and buttoned him up.

"I'm only going across the hall!"

"I'm glad you're only going across the hall." Suddenly they heard a lusty groan from the apartment above. "Dirty old man," tut-tutted Lucasta. "But it cuts both ways: if he can groan loudly and incessantly, we can party loudly and incessantly. Right?"

"Right." agreed Alistair. "Here, I almost forgot..." He rummaged between his sheets for her underwear and handed it to her daintily.

She waved goodbye with it and closed the door of the apartment.

Alistair's mind was reeling still – and getting to like it that way. He pondered the next move. He might ask her out to a French film. Or maybe a Chinese meal. Or a Chinese film followed by a French meal. Or a French film about a couple who go out for a Chinese meal... He felt in his pocket for the keys to his apartment.

No keys. He tried his other pocket, knowing full well they weren't there either. But one must react conventionally at all times, especially if one is a trainee accountant. He hesitated, then walked back across the hall. No sooner had he knocked than the door opened.

"Come in, Alistair," Lucasta greeted him. "Long time no see."

He followed her back into the apartment.

"I've lost my keys, Lucasta. I was wondering if they could have fallen out of my pocket while I was here."

"I'll look but I'm not hopeful."

She rummaged through the pile of his clothes where his jacket had been, but peremptorily. Unlike tissues, apparently, keys don't inspire her to thorough rummages.

"They're not here," she announced, a mere ten seconds later. "What will you do now?" That look again.

"Oh, there's no problem. I'll see the landlady. She's bound to have a spare set knocking around someplace."

Lucasta shook her head. Alistair found himself doing the same, only more slowly.

"Try again, Alistair. The landlady's away for the weekend."

"That's strange, I thought I heard -"

A knock at the door.

"Rats!" exclaimed Lucasta, sweeping past him to answer it.

She opened it and Alistair heard the landlady say:

"I just thought I'd pop my head in to see you're settling in alright, Miss Lyall."

Alistair had the impression that the landlady craned her neck to see inside, but Lucasta wouldn't let her. Unpacked, but nonetheless immoveable.

"You're very kind, but everything's fine."

"Did Roland explain about the garbage? You just –"

"Yes, he told me."

"If there's anything you need –"

"I'll hammer on your door instantly, Mrs. Coyne."

Mrs. Coyne laughed, but still wasn't taking the hint.

"Your neighbour across the hall, Mr. Tick, is ever so pleasant. He's a chartered accountant -"

"Trainee accountant," Alistair heard Lucasta correct her. "But you're right – he's a dote, isn't he? I love the way his eyebrows droop and the way he blushes and that tinkly laugh he has and the sexy way he cycles his bike and ... well, just about everything about him, really. But I'm keeping you: be sure to have a wonderful trip."

"But, my dear, I'm –"

"No, I won't keep you a minute longer with my blathering. Good night, Mrs. Coyne."

And Lucasta shut the door firmly in the landlady's face.

She joined Alistair on the sofa.

"Phew, what a gasbag! I'm glad she's gone, aren't you?"

That look *again*.

"Look, Lucasta, I'd better catch up with her and borrow her keys –"

"Nonsense," declared Lucasta authoritatively. "You couldn't possibly bother her at this hour. Besides –" She cupped her ear. "That's her nephew's car come to pick her up."

Alistair strained his ears, but couldn't hear it. Lucasta cut short his protests.

"No, there's nothing else for it: you'll have to spend the night here."

"But Lucasta –"

"It's no trouble. It's the least I can do after you saved my skimpies from a drenching."

"But Lucasta –"

"I'll make you up a bed in the spare room this instant."

Lucasta was already on her way down the hall.

It suddenly registered that Lucasta had said "spare room". Alistair wasn't sure if he was relieved or disappointed. His mind, reeling for the third time that day, was loving every minute of it. And, once again, he caught the eye of one the calendar-girls. He looked away quickly as Lucasta returned to the sitting-room.

"OK, Alistair, it's all fixed. I go to bed early on Friday night. Don't stay up too late." Then, over her shoulder, "Sleep tight, Alistair Tick - I hope the bedbugs don't bite." She blew him a kiss, then disappeared down the hall.

Resolutely avoiding the calendar-girl's eye, Alistair entered the spare room. A pyjama-top with red stripes rested on his pillow. He undressed and put it on. Only to discover that there were no pyjama-bottoms. He pulled back the bedclothes but found, to his surprise – he was rather surprised to find himself capable of surprise after everything that had happened –that his bed had been apple-pied. He heard a chuckle behind him and turned to see Lucasta standing in the doorway. She was wearing a white dressing-gown, loosely-tied, and pyjama-bottoms with red stripes.

"I wouldn't bother, if I were you," Lucasta advised him, "it's well and truly baked. That was one thing I did learn at the convent ... Forget it, you'd have to strip it completely. Far easier to strip me instead."

She moved closer.

Alistair swallowed. There could no longer be any doubt about Lucasta's intentions. Nevertheless, the would-be chartered accountant in him impelled him to clarify the situation. His mind was still reeling, but had not fallen yet.

"Do you mind if I ask you something first?"

"Anything," she replied generously.

"Would I be correct in thinking you fancy me?"

"Yes. From the moment I rummaged through your pockets. You could even say it was love at first rummage."

"And you aren't here by chance?"

"No. I'm here because you live here."

"How did you know I lived here?"

"I saw it on one of your cards when I frisked you."

"What would you have done if Roland hadn't been moving out?"

"He isn't. I came to an arrangement with Roland. Mrs. Coyne thinks I'm Roland's sister up for the weekend; Roland thinks I'm crazy about him."

"Are you?"

"Of course not, silly – I'm crazy about you."

"And how about your skimpies?" Alistair found he liked the word so he added, "Were your skimpies part of the plan, too?"

"I couldn't be sure you'd bring them in but I had a feeling."

"What if the landlady had beaten me to it?"

"I still wouldn't have fancied her."

"And she's not really going out, is she?"

"She never goes out. You're here long enough to know that."

"What if it hadn't rained?" Alistair probed as thoroughly as Lucasta had rummaged in his jacket-pocket the first time.

"I phoned the weather forecast beforehand."

"But what if I hadn't lost my keys?"

"You didn't lose them." Lucasta took his hand and guided it into the pocket of her dressing-gown. Presently his fingers touched a key-ring he recognized as his own. Lucasta's hand squeezed his and the tenant above chose that moment to groan.

"But how could you be sure – sorry, this is my last question, honest – that I fancied you?"

"You've only got to look at your office memos," whispered Lucasta, moving her mouth within kissing distance. "I can see your superiors' report now... The firm of Ferguson, Hanson & Addison –"

"Hanson, Ferguson & Macauley, actually," Alistair corrected her. Hell, if his mind was going down it was going down fighting.

"...is becoming increasingly concerned about the extraordinary behaviour of one of its trainees, one Alistair Tick." Lucasta's och-aye-the-noo Scottish accent was as thick as the product in the commercial from which it derived. "The lad has taken to returning balance-sheets festooned with Cupid's arrows and figures-of-eight in fetching ring-o'-roses formations. We are sad to report that his condition is deteriorating: today he refused point-blank to perform arithmetical calculations involving numbers which weren't curved, on the grounds that they were 'unfeminine'. Our conclusion? Clearly the lad is in love. We are happy for him, but his days with H, F & M are numbered..."

By this stage Alistair's mind had staggered and fallen. But the ex-trainee accountant was too entranced by Lucasta to hear it. He glanced at her shyly.

"Say it, Alistair," she coaxed him. "Don't be so modest."

"I was just thinking you must want me pretty bad. To go to all this trouble on my account, I mean."

"Yes," corroborated Lucasta, slipping out of dressing-gown and pyjama-bottoms to reveal the panties and suspenders Alistair had taken in off the line, "I do."

...But having smiled, the tall woman passed on. Alistair remembered where he had seen her before – coming out of the apartment across from him the evening before.

He reached inside his jacket-pocket and fished out a tissue. When he had cleaned his hands as best he could he set his bike upright again and mounted it uncertainly. He wobbled left into the street where the offices of Hanson, Ferguson & Macauley were situated. Sure enough, before he had cycled another twenty yards his chain came off again.

Alistair locked his bike in the garage adjacent to the apartments where he lived. It had been a distracting afternoon. The other trainees had ragged him mercilessly about his taste in indelible hand-oils and, after the tall woman's smile, balance-sheets had lost their power to seduce his undivided attention. Eros had begun to creep into his calculations...She had aroused his misgivings about accounting as a career. Before he even woke up two decisions had already been made for him: what time he woke up and what he should wear. He felt old - a round-shouldered accountant in a square hole. He dreaded becoming one of those who found crawling so rewarding they forgot how to walk upright, taking files to bed and emerging with in-growing portmanteaux. Even when they weren't crawling they spent so much of their lives on tiptoe they had practically evolved into a new digitigrade species.

Suddenly a terrific downpour ensued, precipitating Alistair's 100-yard sprint to the back garden to salvage his sheets from the clothes-line. They were drenched by the time he reached them. As were the black panties and suspenders belonging, he presumed, to the latest girlfriend of Roland, in the apartment across from him. Alistair realized as he sprinted back to the apartment entrance that the oil on his hands had begun to explore his sheets. Having climbed the stair, he inserted his key in the lock, squeezed into his apartment with his sodden bundle and kicked the door shut behind him.

Eliza Langland

Rubbing Shoulders in the Lost Treasury

If you played a fair piano, or OK guitar and George Shearing or Eric Clapton ... somebody approachable, top class, asked you to sit in on a session, to play along – what would be the effect on your playing? Chances are you'd improve. I think you'd go on from there to play better than ever before, having rubbed shoulders with the best. If you're outnumbered by higher standards than your own, yours rise to meet their's – theirs don't fall to meet yours.

I'm an actor. Years ago, when the Scottish Theatre Company first opened its door to me it felt like, an invitation to join in, be accepted as I understood it at the time, into the best tradition of a Scottish Theatre. In that rehearsal space was a mix of actors from the longest pedigree to the shortest. I was, relatively, one of the newer fellows but here were performers whom I had, as a youngster, admired from the anonymous dark of the auditorium. They were standing about at coffee break, blethering, offering to make me a coffee, a cup of instant acceptance. I drank mine like a grinning child at a grown up dinner.

Here were young and old, innovation tempered with expertise. And in a modest way there were instances of it happening almost immediately. "Ay, I'll show you. Here." The young man takes the coffee cup while the older one tips himself into a forward roll and springs up, dancing. "You try." The young man, all legs and unbendy muscle looks like he might get the hang of it but it's not for this show, it's just because the two of them are interested in the job. It's a bit of patter handed on for some panto in the future.

I'm all ears at the read-through; the full company sitting script in hand to read the play once through together. We're ranged round in a circle of chairs, there's coffee cups on the floor, a few smokers coralled round a couple of ashtrays. We're an assortment of individuals about to create something whole that will bind us all together. We'll start work and assume the corporate identity of our show, will start looking less and less like a disparate group and more and more like a company. But at this moment the prospect of the task is unnerving. I'm sitting beside an actress I've only ever seen from a distance and she tells me she's hardly had a chance to look at the script. She's not as calm about it all as I'd supposed. I feel less alone. We begin and she gives a reading of more weight, subtlety and power than I would have thought possible at first glance. The grinning child's face is wiped straight. We're playing with the big boys now.

As is often the case, if you get work at all, one job leads to another and on another occasion I was sitting beside this same actress again in BBC Radio Drama, for the read through of a radio play. I was to play her character as a young girl so I found myself watching closely, studying the timbre of her voice, the rhythm of her phrasing.

Again I am fooled by the situation. The mood seems quite casual round this well polished table. We have been served tea and biscuits and we looked like a group of conference delegates in the office-like ambience of the BBC building. Elsewhere in adjoining rooms there are people in suits and serious newsroom activities went cheek by jowl with us. It all seems so removed from the dusty warehouses and draughty rehearsal rooms I'd come to expect.

We begin and she did it again. Dressed like a gorgeous advertisement for a fashion house and with no elaborate preparation I'm aware of, she turns into a miserable complaining, ill old biddy with every emotion, every nuance played to the hilt. And although she pulls no punches we can all see she's got more to give and better nuances to find still. I can't drink my tea or crunch my unfinished biscuit and I notice nobody else does either. She and the others in the corps of the company concentrate so fully they create enough focus and carry us youngsters along, and when you see that concentration up close, done by a time-served expert, you begin to see what the job is really all about.

The work of an actor in Scotland is very varied. We move between stage, television, film, radio, despair, (not to mention temping); yet the 'rubbing shoulders' effect, will most often be felt in the radio studio. The contribution radio has made to the canon of Scottish drama has been very strong and not only in the way it has fostered new writers and new drama. Because of the frequency and volume of its work it brings together actors from all over the profession and creates bonds between us.

And it's fast. A 90 minute play can take three to four days of actors' time to make, a series might engage you for up to only three weeks. You all meet at the read-through, eat lunch together and spend time exchanging tales in the green room between scenes and at coffee break. I know I am not alone in enjoying the good atmosphere and concentration to be found in a radio company and the good working relationship that has grown up amongst those who work together a lot. An unspoken demand is made by the older hands. Keep up. Pick up. Listen and respond. You have to switch quickly in and out of performance mode because of the nature of the medium.

Time is a crucial factor in the work and the management consultants have been out writing reports and demanding cutbacks, applying their bureaucratic solutions to an already honed and disciplined profession. We respond by doing it even quicker and for less money. We were already good at making quick decisions, tackling our roles with a sharp decisiveness. I wonder how far we can be pushed.

We look to the strongest of our elders to lead by example and show how far we can be pushed without dropping our standards. What standards? The ones they have set so far.

It's 10:30am and I'm sitting in a kitchen. It's a small kitchen across the hall from a busy office. I'm in the company of my accountant's earlier client. He's been told I'm a new actor and has stayed back to meet me. I'm sitting in the company of an actor I had seen giving a one man show when I was fifteen. We are alone. He starts to talk about the theatre and makes his points by giving bits of speeches to illustrate. Even at elevenses in a smart, black wool coat, stiff collar and tie, the sort of grab to disarm a tax inspector, this actor can summon tears, give an insight into a performance of great emotional integrity and nurse a cup of coffee at the same time.

My children too? My wife killed too? All my pretty ones? O hell-kite! All!

He grabs my arm. It is preposterous and believable and just plain good. He holds my eyes and lets go my arm.

"Do you think this coffee'll stand warming up or should we get him to make a fresh pot?"

Who? What? He's stopped. He's filling the kettle. The water flows like talent and he turns it off. I'm young and astonished.

In 1994 I went to see a revival of the same show he had done in 1969. I went with the same friends and we're forty now so twenty five years had gone by and there, fresh as new paint, was a show that must have been an early influence; that had made me realise I wanted to act. But there are so many mysteries. You don't know quite how to unravel them. One day, circumstance lets you close enough to start to find out.

Some of the older ones I care about so much will never again be my pals – because I rarely see them any more and my only contact with them was through work. Some of them are from the same generation as my father and for the reasons I'll not see him again, neither will I see them. We all move up a rung and soon we are the ones inviting some keen young trumpet player on to the stage.

It's on the job we learn, rubbing shoulders, being accepted, watching each other in rehearsal, on stage, in front of the cameras. It's being taken aside and told quietly what to do when you forget a line or fluff a bit in a radio script. It's being reassured by one who knows and shares the secret.

Yes we must still disagree with each other and scorn some of the old fashioned ways. Of course! But you need a yardstick to measure yourself by and grow. Who wouldn't like to time a bit of business with Duncan Macrae? There are people around who have done – so there's the way if that's what you want to do... and if the companies you work for employ them.

And that's the problem. When I've had the chance to work with some of the people I've mentioned, it's often been in a radio studio. And indeed it's there I worked recently with one actor who doesn't do theatre any more. Whether by choice or not I am not prepared to ask him; there are expediences that preclude theatre yet permit radio work. Time being one of them. But I am glad of the radio plays that allow us to work together at all. I miss the opportunity the Scottish Theatre Company gave us to assemble a panoply of talent, to create unity. I've found some of it again in Radio and it is, I think, an underappreciated force except by those of us who work in it and by those of us who listen faithfully and I commend it warmly to those who are yet to do either. If I have one request to any new young directors who are currently controlling the Scottish Stage – please invite our oldest, most experienced and well-loved actors into your productions, to work alongside the new exciting talent that's emerging and help keep alive the traditions they shared with their elders in their time.

Hamish Wallochie

Ae Dreich Nicht In Hell

Ae dreich nicht in Hell
wi no much on the tele,
I tak a daunder doon
ti the new Community Ha.
Some poets are in toon
ti launch a new anthology
and gie readings fae their wark.
Ablo the Store knock I meet
wi Adolf and wee Joe.
"Are ye gaun?" I spier,
"For fuck's sake naw,
Ti listen ti thon pish?"
They get me doon the road a bit
till I leave them at the Cross.

On Friday Nicht

On Friday nicht,
the rain deean on the winnock pane,
the wund whustlin ower the roof tiles,
oot ben the coupan o a plastic bin.

A sair greet rises like a wumman in jizzen,
bluid rattlin ower the gless.
Unborn words amang the din—
a cauld front o poetry blawin in.

I Had A Dream O Snawflakes

I had a dream o snawflakes fa'n
sae saftly doon abune the Sun.
Ilk fragile, separate, frostit flooer
amang a brither, sister shooer.

I had a dream o snawflake lives,
mithers and bairns, husbands and wives,
aw meltit thegither as ain
like watter on a winnock pane.

I had a dream o snawflake sowels,
a seamless, flutterin, crystal shawl
o licht and love, an antrin lace
o dancin starns in God's bricht face.

Ghaist Dance

This leid haes nae immunity -
a poem is a puir transfusion.
Happit in an auld and raggit sark
o duin and weel yased wurds,
I maun dae a ghaist dance
ti mak it quick and hale aince mair.

Sae shoot me doon, white man,
sae caw me doon, gin ye daur, critic
     – the spirit o this frettit leid
     is no deed yet.

I Hae Lived

(Shunkaha Napin – Wolf Necklace)

I hae lived ma life in this kinrik,
baith man and boy.
Ma relations dover ower,
deep in the yirth at Kirk o Beath
or lig on the broo o the Liza Brae.
When it is time for me ti fa ti pieces,
I am gaunnae fa ti pieces here.

The Grund Is No Ti Be Bocht

(Tashunka Witko – Crazy Horse)

The grund is no ti be sellt or bocht
whaur oor ain fowk walk and bide.

I Bide

(Shunka Witko – Fool Dog)

I bide on a reservation,
pit here ti see oot ma days.
The Unionist class think of me
as a contemptible, foolish tink.

It maun be that I tak ower much tent
o the Unionist Government.

The Yirth Is Haley Ti Ma Fowk

(Chief Seattle's letter ti President Franklin Pierce, 1854)

There's nane can hae the lift ti buy,
There's nane can hae the sma, blae starns ti sell.
Whit sowel – less fuil jalooses that he hauds the yirth ablo?
The caller air is aucht bi nane
nor is the sparklin watter fae the burn.

The yirth is haley ti ma fowk.

A peewit's greet ower heard abune in March,
a honey – happit, thrummlin bee,
the reeky mirk in a gloamin wuid,
the ghaistly haar ower a snawy morn,
were things aw kent ti ma faither's faithers.
Ilka experience I share wi them is sacrid ti me.

The yirth is haley ti ma fowk.

When The Pine Wuids Tak Fire

(Najinyanupi – the Surrounded)

When the pine wuids tak fire,
see aw the sma greetan animals;
the futrets, mice and tods,
aw runnin and loupan and ettlin ti hide
but girred roond bi flames
wi naewhaur ti gan ti.
Ma freends, that is the wey it is the day
wi us Human Beings.

Thieve of Thieves

*(Moto Gleska – Spotted Bear,
Tatanka Yotanka – Sitting Bull)*

You hae pit oor heids thegither
and flung a blanket ower them.
Whaur there is onything ti be taen
and turned intil gowd – coal·or ile or steel or lives,
ye are aw ower oor land like maggots.
Ye hae cam ti oor land and helped yersel.

Ye hae filled yer ain hoose wi siller at oor expense
while we hae let ye. I hae nae will
ti gan ti your land yet ye cam ti mine.
Oor smeddum has been mined, oor resistance has subsided,
yet ye wonder why we wish ye ill.
Ay the seams o coal lig yonder, aneth Binnertie Hill.

Lane Craw

I greet for the puir craw in the stervan maw o Winter,
hingan ti his cauld bare tree, that still he could be deid.
In Februar, I wonder at whit wersh and dreary thochts
gae through his sma black heid.

Ti The Human Beings

Noo ye hae gan as the bears hae gan
fae the ancient wuids o Caledon,
as the buffalo fae the tuim and wheat fu prairies.
Ye hae left ahint a guid mindin
and taen yer fauts wi ye.
I dae not believe in the White Man's myths,
yet I dae believe in yours.
Whaur I live the day on Hell Reservation
it's faur easier for me ti sleep wi ma heid in a dream state
than ti be waukrife in the ane I'm in.

Yet aince in nae dream time,
a souch o wind blew a great green wave o tree taps
fae Sutherland aw the wey ti Galloway
and in atween were bison, elk and boar,
while reid tungued wolves schauchled ben
like grey ghaists in the pale green licht.

On a Summer's dawin, deep in sleep, I am back there,
in that still and lang gan airt.
Sae why no you here,
Dead Eyes and Running Antelope?

Ye hae taen yer fauts wi ye, Great Warriors,
and left a memrie o humanity.
Gin ye were here wi me,
we could mibbe celebrate Life,
for it is guid ti aye rax ti the guid.

Let us drink a dram in ma wigwam hoose,
blaw a pipe in Blairadam Wuids.

I Loo The Colours...

I loo the colours o the leid I scrieve in;
gowden, blae and crammasie.
I tak nae tent o form or reason
when words cam fleean, tapsilteerie.

This bletheran skite is moved bi the Muse,
stouned bi the magick o words, I pent
Life in the thirldom o rhyme, I choose
ti mak nae sense and experiment.

The Spirit o makkin is blindin and bricht,
I'm fu fae the word – well whaur its drawn,
I hae fan intil a world o licht
wi Herbert, Crashaw, Marvell and Vaughan.

Ti The Great Spirit

Ye are the ane and ma ain, the ane that is ayeweys aye,
Ye are the aw: tho I am sma, aw that is no is nane.
I am naethin and awthin, a pairt,
a thocht, a breith, a beat o the hert.
Because o you
I will say aye.
I will say aye till I cannae speik mair,
I will say aye till ma tongue is sair,
Till ma hert is still and ma mind is stouned,
Till ma banes are lourd and lig in the grund,
I will say aye.

A Dreich Nicht In Hell – Pairt Twa

Things hae changed a lot in Hell,
these days ye widnae ken the place ata;
the pits are lang shut, the steel fires gan oot
but there's poetry on at the Community Ha.

Sae I thole aw the talk, drink the free beer
but I'm faur ower thrawn ti shut up and gan hame.
I dinnae ken whit I'm daein here
but I'll say ma piece, aw the same.

Ye see like, friend, I'm no being offensive but
there's something wrang like
no richt, ye ken?
Ocht – it's no the wey ye talk or luik,
Christ! I'm no ane o they reservationists
that want ti fecht ye or tak coup because yer a stranger.
I'm a civilised man, ye ken? I dae work.
I ken it's no your faut
gin ye changed yer accent at university,
no, it's no that... and it's no that I dinnae appreciate Art
either... I'm a scriever in a sma wey masel...
and it's clever, aye, but it's clever the things that ye say.
Yer ideas are bricht, sherp as a spade edge,
and ye yase them ti delve ablo the surface o modern life,
(tho how deep's that?)
yer no parochial either – not a bit o it!
And see yer allusions? They were that guid...
I think ye must ken abidy's place in Hell's literary tradition
and yer ain place in relation ti it aw
as if ye had measured it ti the very inch.
And talk aboot satirical? Man, ye were that sarcastic!
Naw, yer nae Hellyairder, you,
I can even see yer regional voice being published ootside Hell.
Naw, I hope yer no takkin it ti hert whit I'm sayin...
I can see bi yer face that yer no,
But there's juist ane, sma thing...

Why dae ye never write poetry?

Jim Brunton

Twa Hymns

1 Fur the Hairst

We ploo the fiels an mainner
nitrets by the tin.
Oor beasts ur fed wi hormones
an nivver glimp the sin.
We eik the lift wi pushin
sae thet nae burds twit;
an tant the thrawart tounies
thet weird o pine an smit.

A Goad's gifts aroon us —
it disna maitter which,
we roup Him oot,
we roup Him oot,
tae mak us rich.

2 Intercession

Faither for aye, lat oor braw
fushers sile Yir ilka swaw
an herrie thoosands fush a shot,
sae wee — juist settin fir tae rot:
      O, hear us whan we greet tae Thee
      fur thae gowdhowkwers oan Yir sea!

O, Treenity, gie thaim the pooers
tae scrach wi screengers a the oors
and lat thaim scart Yir nor-sea grund
til a Yir craiturs are nae mair fund:
      O, hear us whan we greet tae Thee
      fur thae gowdhowkers oan Yir sea !

O Christ, gie a Yir glimmerin dauds
tae thaim oor naitions aye uphauds;
see's us weys tae kepe thaim stoot
yince thai've kilt Yir pout an poot:
      O, hark tae us greetin tae Thee
      fur thae gowdhowkers oan Yir sea !

"Contra nando incrementum"

Fechtin the flude,
Am naebody's craitur;
res nullius in coort —
belangin tae nane.
But gin tak a flee,
a laird's ma maister
tae grill or poach me
in a different kettle.

Breaking the Rules

Yvonne D Claire

This time it would be all right. Faces and number-plates were like cyphers: once decoded, everything fell into place. Neatly. She'd learnt how to do it, and no mistake. Despite her parents' warnings, their threats and tears. She was her own mistress now; other people's paranoia didn't matter any longer. Of course, if she'd wanted to, she could have made the train home to Anders. She could have run and the summer heat would have left her all limp and sticky. The leather seats, scarred with roughly stitched-up crosses, would have pressed into her bum and thighs like open sores.

And then the kids. Schoolkids. Always blocking the aisles and bragging about their petty deceptions, their cleverness. Such cheats. *She* knew all about that sort of thing. About inside soles sweaty with mathematical probabilities. Stocking tops guarding the laws of economics or the secret of the earthworm's sex-life. She knew about fresh paper hankies which, held close to your face for that irrepressible sneeze, would suggest rose-water and the delicate ramifications – past, present and future – of *aimer* in different moods.

It was mid-afternoon, and the streets quite empty. The lunchtime down-pour had left a string of puddles along the kerb that winked at her every time she turned her head. In the nearest, streaks of petrol were slinking out as colours of the rainbow. Pretty enough. Pity about the sky though, its vastness all soiled into ragged patches of blue and wispy white. With the tip of her umbrella she ripped open the surface, swirled the water, scoured the stone until there was a squelch and she saw the mirror go blind.

Some of the muck had splashed over her sandals. She wriggled her toes – how delicious dirt could be! – then bent down hastily with a crumpled-up train ticket and began to rub. Scraping the skin red and sore. Still scrap-ing when she heard it; a low growl that suddenly exploded into a roar as the motorbike rounded the corner of Station Avenue. She straightened up, flicked back her hair. No need to put her thumb out just yet because of the lights further down. She'd let the bike pull up before flashing a smile towards the visor.

Well done. And the driver was right on cue too with his left hand raised lazily to acknowledge her. Fumbling with the strap under his chin in shy awkwardness. So, should she accept? His vehicle looked great, chrome-plated and everything, like one of those choppers in *Easy Rider*. Not that she'd have much chance of getting a decent conversation going. But it would be different. Exciting. With the slack air twirling into eddies round their bodies, and her legs as smooth and cool as marble –

Shit. The lights had changed, and there he was turning left, not even bothering to indicate, only the smear of his teeth trailing behind. What a sham. Playing hide and seek, was he? Not with her, no, thank you. Past the bank, the supermarket, past the school, disappearing behind the

police-station, gathering speed now and racing uphill towards the ceme-
tery, not giving a damn whether he blasted the flowers on the graves.
Thought himself king of the road, did he? Well, she could hardly see him
any more. Fading along the gloom of trees and tall old houses into a mere
fly's buzz. King of the road? Sod him.

How rigid she'd become. Achingly tense. If she was at the office she'd
make a dash for the toilet and, with her back against the wall, fall to frig-
ging herself. Out here, all she could do was ravage her nails. To hell with
the unchipped coral pink. The little finger first.

Those women were taking ages to waddle by. Craning their necks with
their beaks almost touching. What did they mean, parking their shopping
bags in front of the photographer's window? None of *their* pictures on
show in there, that was for sure. Unless they were watching her reflection,
of course ... Huh, she'd give them the time of their lives. She moved her
hands up and down her body, shuddered and spat bits of nail into the
puddle where the rainbows had reformed.

Nothing more soothing than being a little rude sometimes. The two
hags had beaten it, and all she wanted to do now was close her eyes, keep
them closed for as long as possible, and let the tugs of pain at her finger-
tips merge with the sunlight burning under her lids.

Several cars had slowed to a *purr-purr*, and their windows eased down.
She didn't care, not any longer; she wasn't that desperate. The squeaky
frames were the worst, giving her the creeps before she heard the usual:
"Hey darling, let's go for a ride!" or "Want to earn some money, honey?"

How about that electric swish a second ago? Brisk and crisp as a busi-
nessman, and the driver sounded quite genuine: "Can I help you, young
lady? Are you all right?" Such clinging concern, though. Boring her stiff
already. She yawned with her mouth open. Like that toddler asleep on the
bus the other day. His mother had been pestering him, prodding and jab-
bing and hissing his name. But he'd merely pushed her away, his lip all
curled. How weary he'd seemed, how indifferent; not a single glance
towards the bunch of kids with their bird-cage or the old woman across
the aisle who'd moaned on about being 'sick of shadows' or something.
He, at least, had learnt self-control. Lucky little devil.

"You hitching?" A deep voice.

"Yeah —" She blinked, "Thanks for stopping." This one was wearing
cowboy boots, and his eyes were different colours – greenish-grey and
light brown. A posh blue Audi. But what about his number-plate? She
couldn't see it. The car had come to a halt right beside her, and she hadn't
bloody noticed. She must be stricter with herself. Readiness was all:
"Where're you heading?" Perhaps he'd lost one of his contact lenses.
Shouldn't she check his number-plate, decode it? Her hands were clammy.
It would be a relief to get out of the sun.

"Anders. I can drop you off near the centre if you like." He smiled at her.

He was chatty and easy-going. A good omen. She'd better ignore his
eyes, forget about the number-plate. "Suits me fine," she smiled back, wip-

ing her hands on her dress. Diagonally behind the car the wooden walls of the station had weathered into the sheen of raw silk. The next train was due in less than a quarter-hour.

He called himself Tony. Said he was a commercial artist with his own small firm. That he liked computer games and country music. Had taught himself guitar. Loved preparing food for guests, played squash, and sometimes had a pint or two. She'd met his type before.

Why didn't he want to discuss his friends and family? So pigheaded. Always chipping away "And you, what do you do?"

Eventually she found herself telling him about the clothing company. About phoning and faxing and feeding her Mac. About dealing with complaints like worn elastics, fraying selvages, faults in the dye – child's play, really, once you knew your customers. Today had been sales statistics on men's underwear: "Bet you prefer ordinary Vs? No fancy pants for you, eh?" She burst into giggles.

"Can you drive?"

She shrugged, "Sort of, I'm still a learner ..."

"Enjoy it?"

"Oh, yes –" Wait a minute; hadn't his tone become sharper, almost teacherly?

"Get much practice?"

This was definitely turning into an interrogation. But she wasn't at school any more. Not her. She could see the river now, glittering brokenly through a line of black poplars on the near bank.

"Do you get much practice?"

She made no reply.

"Just wondering, that's all."

The grin in his voice hadn't escaped her. Bugger him. With her teeth clenched, she kept staring straight ahead until her eyes felt strained and raw, and the road seemed to be rushing in on her. The sunglasses, quick. Her eyes were watering really badly.

"Would you like a go then?"

The little case flew open with a snap: "What? Me? You must be joking!" Why should he want to risk getting his car wrecked? And without knowing her? Once at the wheel, of course, she wouldn't be able to fight back, and he might do all kinds of things: slide his hands inside her dress, touch her breasts, or maybe even touch himself ...

"I'm not sure –" she adjusted her glasses.

"No strings attached, if that's what you're worried about." A pathetic attempt at coughing, then: "I have full insurance, you know."

She thought he'd darted a glance at her out of the corner of his greenish-grey eye, and for an instant she studied him curiously. His gaze fixed on the road, he never batted an eyelid, and the fringes on his right boot hung suspended in two perfect semi-circles as he kept his foot down.

They'd reached the bridge. Against the water's glare the poplars appeared bleached and ineffectual. His generosity was a bit too good to be true. A cover-up, most probably. So what? Why should she feel under any obligation? It was *his* suggestion, after all. And if he did become over-friendly, she'd threaten an accident. Nothing like blackmail.

"As long as you don't mind arriving home late; I'm not very fast. . ."

He brought the car to a standstill on the grass verge.

He'd started on about his job again. She only half-listened, heard him mention labels and logos. Computer-aided graphics. Colour simulation on the screen — whatever that meant. Must be married to his work, poor sucker. But hang on, what was this he'd said just now? About maybe showing her round his firm? No reason for him to do so, really. Anyway, she ought to concentrate on her driving; they were approaching the vine-yards up-river, and the road was narrowing with some nasty bends.

He drizzled on. A zig-zag, and she hadn't used the brakes once. The secret was changing gears at precisely the right moment. And power-steering. She felt great. Everything was under control: the road, the car, the afternoon. Tony.

All of a sudden he said to go right. The winery? What for? She didn't want — No —

"Hey, I explained a minute ago I'd have to hand in a couple of designs for bottle labels up there. Nice hairpin bends, too."

Some challenge! The lane squirmed through the vines like a caterpillar drunk on the smells of earth, stone and dry wood. Tony was silent all the way to the estate. As he was reaching for his briefcase on the back seat she heard him gabble the old cliché about taking things easy. "Yes," she said. "And you."

She woke with a start; Tony was tapping at the window. Decent enough, considering. Because he could have sneaked in and — She gave him a quick smile.

"Had a good nap? Christ, what a furnace!" he recoiled in mock-horror then, briefcase in one hand, door in the other, swung them to and fro rap-idly a few times before climbing in beside her.

She bowed: "Thanks for the refreshment, sir."

They both laughed, and she switched on the ignition as if the car was hers. It seemed natural to ask how he'd got on.

"Fine. The manager was so taken with my ideas he promised me some complimentary bottles of this year's harvest. Come to think of it, I might let you have one — in return for your taxi services."

This was the beginning of July, and the grapes weren't even ripe yet. Without turning her head she mumbled how very nice.

He shifted in his seat, "Well, what about yourself? Enjoy hitching?" A sec-ond's hesitation. "Pretty dangerous for a girl on her own, I'd imagine."

What was he trying to insinuate? She changed down, indicated and rejoined the traffic on the river road. Neat job, but he hadn't even noticed. Not one single word of praise. Taking her for granted already. Not enough that she was chauffeuring him round the countryside, oh no, monsieur also expected to be entertained. So that was why he let her drive his car; he wanted her to trust him, wanted to worm his way into her good graces.

Hadn't he moved again? Manoeuvring his body closer to hers, was he? She jerked away. Never mind the swerve, the opposite lane wasn't busy. He was yawning, but she'd heard him gasp all right. That should teach him. She grinned and went faster, overtaking a 2 CV decorated with giant ladybirds.

He was leaning towards her, his green eye almost black, "Slow down, please. No need to break the speed limit."

She let the needle drop, "I was merely testing the car." A farmhouse passed in a blur, its windows ablaze with geraniums or begonias. "Not bad, really." The road was less wriggly now, cutting across a patchwork of cornfields, woods, and orchards with dun cattle behind wire fences. Why didn't he speak? Worse than that little boy on the bus. Had he gone deaf, or dumb, perhaps? His shoulders stooped, his face was blank.

The air seemed to have grown hotter. White heat like liquid glass. Soon it would be crystallizing round her. Smothering her. She should say something. Get him loosened up. A story. She'd tell him a story. Her throat made a rasping noise: "Once upon a time a man offered a girl a lift. He had a smart number-plate, was bright and cheery, and began cracking jokes that made the girl shake with laughter. Gradually, however, he changed his tune ..."

How she hated roadworks – and the light had just turned red. She glanced over at Tony. Still no change: a stuffed dummy. What was the matter with him? She gripped the wheel harder and waited for the green light. When it came on she accelerated with a screech, stalling the car. Someone hooted.

"You left it in third gear." Tony's voice.

"I know," she said. "Of course I bloody know," she repeated a little louder. "Anyway, it's your fault. You distracted me –" Sweat was trickling down her forehead, eating into her eyes. No air-conditioning. Christ, what a crappy car. "You can do the talking from now on. Tell me about yourself. No more recipes, computer games or country music, understand?" Her hair was such a mess, all damp and sticky. She wiped her hand on the upholstery, then pulled the gear lever straight down. The engine revved.

"If you stop at the next lay-by, I think I'll –"

Second instead of fourth. "Something wrong with that fucking gearbox." Had he heard her? There were dribbles of sweat running down the sides of her nose, searing the corners of her mouth. He should be worried, for fuck's sake, get it sorted out.

"Well, it's never caused me any problems. Anyway, you've done enough driving for today, let's just. . ."

Smartarse. "'Never caused me any problems.' Huh. So what *are* your problems, sunny boy, tell me?" The taste of salt on her tongue, sickening. . .

"In here!" His arms were flailing.

Even if her head was near to bursting, she was playing it real cool. Yet another sloping bend and hardly a skid. She was doing fine. That bastard on his motorbike couldn't have zoomed through it any faster.

"Stop it, OK? Stop the car!"

"What? You don't want to talk, is that it? First have me do all the work, then ditch me?" She'd show him. She wouldn't let go; he'd have to prise her fingers apart like clams, every single one of them. Gritting her teeth, she pulled the wheel closer – closer still. Yes, she'd show him all right. But the wheel seemed so slippery all of a sudden; and why was it beginning to twist and turn in her hands? Why was it making those faces at her, such ugly, leering faces? She couldn't bear –

When she opened her eyes the car had stopped, her door was ajar and the seatbelt unfastened - no harm done. Tony was sitting by the roadside, his head on his knees. What a wimp. She got out, feeling much better already, and went across. She took off her sunglasses, but he didn't even look up, simply sat there, reeking of self-pity. Without a word she jangled the keys over him.

"Please –" he began and raised his eyes. They were the same colour at last, almost black. She smiled, "You just don't understand, do you?" A few steps towards the car, a playful little wave, then she drew back her arm.

The keys caught the sun before they fell somewhere in the high grass. "Safe journey home!" Another wave. No more worries about his number-plate now, or his contact lenses. She grinned and kept walking.

Peter McCarey

Ten Petrarchan Sonnets in a Khosian Click Language

(Ten or was it zen, Petrarchan as in written on the heart,
sonnets, sonatas, things that sound
in a place where hunters whisper)

The sky was the usual southern mess,
the Cross was down and Canopus rising;
meteorites came crashing into time.
A lonely Chinese restaurant
talk of work and family, time,
the good of verse, analysis,
I didn't see the danger
the spoor of creatures figured in the sky
at noon that lick their paws in the heart
of a candlepod acacia.

At the grave of David Livingstone's infant daughter in the ruins of their house near Gaborone

Lisa, Lizzie, Betsy, Beth,
a stony dream, an early death,
your mummy's gone and this is the hand that rocks you.

Elizabeth in this place
the full futility of talking
has dried my lips until they crack in song.

Paludrine

"You have a sense of the absurd, but you don't like the absurd."

Well I don't think I was bitten
and transmission's slow in winter
and there's drug-resistant strains there anyway,
so I stopped taking the pills, my wee Pals,
because they cloud the vision
and dull the hearing, and disable
my Houdini sense of humour,
which I need now. Besides,
what's good enough for Dante and MacDiarmid
will do for me.

Sophia

"We believe what eases our minds"

Before Martha was Martha
before Martha was born
in crystal Geneva
I heard a ship's horn
bring in the New Year;

I heard hundreds of vessels
that weighed on the Clyde,
that my grandfather plated
and my father sighed over
at work. Can you hear it?

A jig on the pedals
of thirty-foot pipes!
Here, open the window –
frost in the pines :
we were 500 miles from the water.

I was 500 mile from the ocean
where a great river runs
out of steam, out of breath
in a wheeling and rusting
and shuddering life.

I'd just chased a wolf-spider
from under my net,
I'd got under the blankets
and put out the light
when I heard them - all

the gougers and biters,
anaesthetists, all
that the bats couldn't glean
from the thatch or the wall,
and I waited.

Now the south wind draws snow
from the Drakensberg Ridge
and the rains can come fast
as the plummeting edge
of a snake-eagle's wing.

Well it drowned out their chatter
and maybe drowned them,
and I slept like a babe.
It was wind in the palms,
wind in the branches

and clattering leaves.
I was far from the ocean
and miles from the sea
but I thought I heard You...

Happy the Pure in Heart

Two of us were standing at the office door
when here comes Sorgho down the corridor
looking like he's making headway
against a strong south-westerly.
"Heureux les coeurs purs" he snapped, and on he went.
By and by he's coming back,
still shouldering into that wind.
"Now who was that intended for?"
"Moi-même" he grinned, head down. Well brother, maybe,
but given your track record
you have to mean pure crazy.

****

Stuffing a payphone on the border
for some place five-and-a-half time zones away
to clicks and pauses that gulp numbers
as limbic signals drop from one
expectancy to none -
linoleum
in limbo
and my hands have lost their memory.

Who let this mind in armour lance my heart?
What law empowers reason to abort
so nothing good or bad can come of it?
Is intellect the enemy,
that undermines but doesn't understand?
I know my mind; I want to know my heart.

Well it looks like butchered bagpipes, and it feels
like they've been stepped on, but
it dunders the beat
like a Strathclyde Police pipe band.

The Firefinch (M.C.)

Smokey's after the firefinch. Listen, cat :
you touch that bird and you'll be feeding
the Gucci golfbags in the creek.
I love it more than all the flocks
that cross the desert with the clouds.
It's molten rock, the tiny
pulse of possibility. It is
the loving breath that breathes on me.

Nearly there. Now you've recovered faster
than from flu or any faint
indisposition.
There's nothing can crack your heart
when you don't own one :
you're a Christian saint,
you're a Zen master.

All or None

The fact, discovered by Bowditch,
that the heart muscle, under whatever stimulus,
will contract to the fullest extent or not at all

— Dorland's Medical Dictionary

There's collarbones like hickory wands,
fine as fanstruts on a soundboard,
patient as wingstruts, fuselage
to vellum stretched on a warping frame.
I could lock you away in this desk drawer
with nothing but the desk drawer key for company.
God knows why I put up with you. God knows
why a woman should take the weight
the aches and murmurs of a husband.

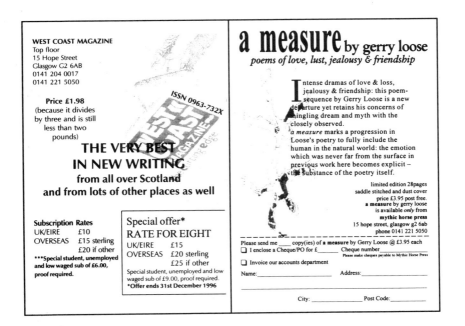

Talking it Over With Genghis Khan

Heather Reyes

When Eva first learned about wars and things, she thought she'd better start going to church – just in case. If you prayed hard enough, you were supposed to get your own way. Like 'no more wars'. If that was the case, it seemed a pity that not enough people in the past had bothered. But she was Eva and used to getting her own way.

To one side of the chapel of Our Lady of the Immaculate Conception, Jesus pointed to a sort of Valentine's card on his chest – a big red heart with different length sun-rays coming out of it. But he didn't look particularly pleased about getting the card. A bit sad, really. Opposite him, a lady in blue and white smiled down sweetly at the snake she'd trodden on ... The candles around her were crying themselves away. Between the two, above the altar, yellowy white and hanging heavily from the nails, the awful body. The vermilion droplets, so red and so many, made her think of nosebleeds, and then of a procession of bishops across old snow. But the red copes of the bishops burst into machine-gun fire, and then turned back to blood as the soldiers died in the snow. And all the suffering people began pouring out of the wound in Christ's side. No wonder the other Jesus didn't look too impressed with the Valentine's card: there wasn't really much love about at all, to judge from what was coming out of His side.

If you waited in the quiet of the empty church, waited, and watched the great wound beneath the ribs, Time ran backwards and you saw nearly two thousand years' worth of tortured, suffering people trailing out of it like a ragged column of mutilated ants. And if you waited and waited, in the end you'd see Him stagger out of His own side, stumbling under the great cross – only it would be little, all the people very little, seen from a long way off so the particularities of their wounds and mutilations and sadnesses were reduced by Time and not so upsetting, like turning the telescope round and looking through the wrong end to push everything far, far into the minuscule distance. But, even at that remove, she could see them stretching out their tiny arms to her.

Then a sudden close-up. People dragging themselves out of the mud as they were – torn, rotting, showing a piece of cheekbone, the knob of a shoulder-joint, red trickling from the corners of what was once a mouth and from the nose-spaces. They crawled towards her, dragging themselves forward for her to heal and mend and soothe, and to have her tell them it didn't really happen, that History was only a bad dream that all the world had dreamed at the same time.

She started with the soldiers, working the shreds of flesh back onto the faces like a sculptor pressing globs of clay on to build up a head, sucking out the bullets like mammoth bee-stings, and sending them all home to their wives and mothers and children whose black clothes she took off, dressing them instead for a celebration and putting flowers everywhere.

It took a lot of time and concentration to do all that. They couldn't make

Illustration by Stephen Lee

out why she'd turned so quiet and strange at home. They suspected it was something to do with this going to church business. And it was exhausting work, too, persuading Herod not to kill all those babies, calming Genghis Khan down, and trying to convince Hitler, "Look, you're not going to win, you know". It meant hours and hours in your own room, growing paler and paler – except beneath the eyes.

She began to develop her own theory that the thugs of History were really all the same person reborn at different times. Well, they all seemed to have moustaches. Obviously thought they were 'real men' – or suspected they weren't and were trying to ... Anyway, whichever one you were trying to reason with, it felt like the same as all the others – except Genghis Khan's clothes were more interesting. If they *were* all the same person, then she could just choose one manifestation and try talking it over with him – the dead babies, the Jews ... everything. She'd choose Genghis, of course; more exotic to look at. Better than just a Charlie Chaplin in uniform.

She had him sitting there for hours, cross-legged on her bed, while she paced up and down the pink fluffy carpet, and him having to take his furs off because of the central heating so that all his gold chains and stuff hung on his ever-so-hairy chest and his purple and orange baggy trousers clashed with the pink bedspread.

"Don't you understand? People are going to hate you for *ever*. History will..."

And sometimes, try as she might to keep him Genghis his flying moustachios would shrink and he'd become jerky, beady-eyed little Hitler.

"How *could* you...?!"

Once she made *him* sit there while she read the whole of *The Diary of Anne Frank* to him, even though it took until two in the morning and she dozed off during maths the next day. She'd begun to believe she was getting somewhere with him – them – though you couldn't be sure, of course. But anything was worth a try.

Sometimes she looked around the class and wondered if anyone else was talking to Genghis Khan or any of them, and whether she could ask for help with mending the soldiers. Even if she managed one a day for the rest of her life, she'd never get through a fraction of those poppy petals falling from the roof of the Albert Hall. And that was just for a *couple* of wars. But she realised there wasn't much chance, not in that class, anyway. You only had to listen to them talk.

The thing she found most difficult to understand was how, after the Renaissance and the Enlightenment and the other big ideas Miss Wheatcroft had gone on about, there should still be people killed for their colour, their religion, or what they did with words. So many hurt bodies. Each of us living on a hill of hurt bodies. Let alone minds. That was to come.

As she walked to church early on Easter morning – grey, dank, and not at all hopeful, crows circling the still bare tree-tops – she wondered if many people got muddled up between Renaissance and Resurrection, like Nancy Goodrich always did ('always' meaning twice, really). Renaissance was a nicer word. Prettier clothes went with it – coloured velvets, pearls, ruffs, embroidery, gold thread. Resurrection didn't have much more than grubby old sheet-things draped round the people. There'd probably be old blood-stains or something, too. And all that dust in the creases. In Religious Instruction Mrs Legg had talked about the rebirth of Nature and Hope in the Spring and how it was no coincidence that Easter was...

She'd sat there, wondering why you didn't use Renaissance about Nature, only boring old 're-birth'. Of course, Renaissance was supposed to be all paintings and old books and stuff. But it was such a lovely word she decided she'd start a fashion for using it about the bulbs coming up again so miraculously, and pink bursting from the dead-looking apple-tree twigs.

By this time she was passing the park with the playground where she'd fallen off the slide when she was seven. But it had gone now. So had the old green-slatted roundabout with the huge, red-painted knob in the middle that was so hot to hold onto in the summer and so achingly cold in the winter. The park was being remodelled, being brought 'up to date', and having the drainage done, too. There were still several huge concrete pipes that hadn't been used.

Somebody moved in the bushes. Eva looked around, feeling alone and visible in the grey morning. No-one else was out walking so early. If it was a murderer, she'd have to try one of her Hitler-type conversations on him, persuade him he'd be a lot happier – and so would everyone else – if...

From the bushes there emerged a woman in an old-fashioned green coat and a felt hat kept on with a pearl-ended hat-pin. Her hands were clasped across her stomach and a cream plastic handbag hung from her right forearm. The grass was muddy and her heels kept sinking in, making her walk look clumsy and uncertain.

She reached one of the concrete pipes, stopped, and looked around as if checking she was alone. A crow flew over, slowly, as crows do, making a sound like a laugh in slow motion. Eva kept very still. The woman manoeuvred herself onto her knees at the entrance to the pipe, then disappeared inside. She must be looking for something. But how did she know it was in the pipe? She couldn't have dropped it there herself. Women like that didn't go in pipes.

Eva walked closer so that she could see right in. The woman was on her side, making struggling movements with her arms and legs every now and then. And slowly, very slowly, she was edging her way through the pipe. From time to time she seemed to be looking at her watch.

Eva wondered if she should call an ambulance.

Then she was through. She stood up briefly and pulled something brown out of her handbag, which she had kept hold of all the time. Unfolding it, she spread the brown thing on the ground, dropped to her knees again, then awkwardly got herself down and onto her back.

It was then that the awful crying started – a comedian taking off a baby, but also a man on fire.

Remembering the broken glass that was often all over the playground, Eva ran to bind the woman's wounds. This was a real woman, real wounds. She only wished she had more than one handkerchief with her.

The woman was a tortoise on its back, limbs working like a tipped over clockwork toy. Her face was puckered, but the vermillion mouth was open wide and there was the white bulge of flesh between the stocking-tops and the knickers warm over the crotch.

Eva stood beside her now, looking down. The red mouth snapped shut. The eyes opened, disbelieving, then afraid, and only after the years and years of the five seconds for which they looked at each other did the woman's face dissolve into embarrassment and guilt.

"Are you alright?" Eva made herself say. The woman sat up and reached for the cream handbag, now smeared with mud. "I thought you'd hurt yourself. There's often broken glass. Sorry if I made you jump."

"It's alright", said the woman, getting up ungracefully. "You didn't really spoil it. I'd done the main part already."

"Main part of what?"

"The treatment. I read about it in a magazine, thought it might help: all those doctors. 'Reliving the birth process' they called it. I've had my eye on these pipes for ages. And it had to be ten to eight – that's the time I was born."

"On Easter Day?"

"No...October."

"It doesn't matter about the date, then; just the time?"

"I'm not sure, now you mention it. Perhaps you're right. Perhaps that's why I don't feel different – well, not very."

"You don't feel better?"

"It might be too soon to tell. These deep things take their time."

Eva thought of all the hours she'd spent mending soldiers. She scanned the woman's body quickly. It must be internal injuries, then.

"What is it that's wrong with you?"

"They tell me it was the Blitz – being cuddled by a dead mother for a day before they dug me out. They say I've never been quite right in the head since. But it's difficult for me to know. I mean, what are other people like in the head? I was only three at the time." She bent down, picked up the sheet of brown paper, refolded it and pushed it back into her handbag. "Didn't want to get my coat dirty", she said, brushing the skeleton of a leaf from her sleeve. "I'll go back now." But she stood still, looking at the pipe.

After a few moments, Eva thought she'd better remind her about going back, and take the opportunity of using her word, too. She said, "I hope you feel better ... for your *Renaissance* ... when you get back."

"Oh – yes – back. Thank you."

Eva was disappointed. The woman didn't bat an eyelid at the word. Never mind. She could try it on someone else – it just seemed such a perfect opportunity.

The woman turned and began to walk away, crookedly, over the oozy grass. There was laughter from the pond: the ducks had woken up.

"So," thought Eva, "it's worse than I thought. It's minds as well as bodies. I'm going to give that Genghis a real piece of my mind tonight." She sighed wearily and dragged herself on towards the church.

After the service she knelt there, as usual, looking at the three of them - Jesus of the Valentine, His snake-squashing mummy, and big dead Jesus. A tiny woman in a green coat crawled out from under His ribs, catching her handbag on the side of the wound.

"I could do with a bit of help," Eva said. "It's a bit much expecting me to do it all. I don't mind having a go at the things I can see, but I'm not a psychiatrist."

Jesus stretched, looking surprised to see the Valentine's card in his hand, turned it over curiously, shrugged, and tossed it over His shoulder. Mary said "Stay!" firmly to the snake – thought better of it, removed her white veil, popped the half-dead creature in it, tied it up and kicked it into the corner.

Eva stood up.

"We thought you'd never ask", said Jesus.

"Ten-four: let's go", said Mary.

Eva paused and looked hopefully towards the crucifix.

"Not a chance", said Mary. "It'll be a reminder, anyway."

Eva couldn't help wishing their clothes were a bit more striking and their faces less plastery looking. Would they cut any ice with Genghis Khan?

A passing bag-lady saw a girl and two statues walk out of the church. Eva noticed her and called out, "Don't worry. Everything'll be alright soon. There's going to be a Renaissance!"

The bag-lady paused, broke into a cackling laugh and continued, as before, towards the litter-bin she'd just spotted on the next lamp-post.

W.N. Herbert

Featherhood
(for Debbie)

1

God speaks in sic undeemis weys
that maist o whit he seys
gaes maunderin awa
in prirrs an pirlies lyk
a speugie soomin thru a hedge,

or thi soond o an ice-cream van
prinklin uts notes thru a gloamin estate
in Stranraer,
in the middle o Januar:

ut seems ut maun be meagrims till
He talks ti you in pain
an the meisslin awa o pain,
in solace and
uts meisslin awa.

undeemis - extraordinary; maundering - sounding indistinctly; pirrs an pirlies - gentle breaths and small things; speugie - sparrow; soomin - swimming; prinklin - bubbling; meagrims - absurd notions; meisslin - wasting imperceptibly

2

This is thi wey Eh didnae ken
why thi flaffin flicht
o three grey wullie-wagtails
straicht
in front o ma car
filld me wi mair nor fricht

until
parkd in Castle Douglas
Eh thocht o the computer's
photie o wir ain three eggs
abstractit fae yir boady
an fertilized
by IVF:

that tho yirdit in
yir willin wame
came loose
an flew awa.

flaffin - a fluttering of the wings; yirdit - earthed

3

An kennan this repleyed
thae ithir flee's-wing instants,
nearly stills:

o starin thru a screen intil
thi ocean o yir kelder
lyk a submariner
lukean fur the sonar ding
o wir twa-munth dochtir's
foetal hert;

o sittan in
thi doctir's oaffice
hearan hoo an acronym -
a D & C - wad dae
tae waash awa
hir kebbit pearl

an lukean oot thi windie
at a white plastic bag
risin past oor
second storey,
a flinricken escapin.

flee's wing - very small or short; kelder - womb; kebbit - stillborn;
flinricken - weak person, very thin cloth, a mere rag

4

Here wiz thi sentence, then:
thi three, ma pearlie, and
wan mair simple daith,
his reid refusal tae be held -
gin ut wiz a he -
past mair nor a week o wir kennan:

mebbe ut wiz
a refusal tae be kent
lyk God's refusal tae prevent
thon previous collision
arrehvin in thi Haugh o Urr
atween meh car
an a jenny-wren:

sae sma a plosive
set this up
by silencing that sang,
sae haurd tae ken
God means yi as
his punctuaishun.

5

Sae licht thi lives that laive us
oor griefs maun grow insteed;
thi anely wean
a man can cairry's
absence inniz heid.

But leese me oan thi lea-laik-gair
that spelt me oot this speech,
thi sma hills o thi Stewartry
sae saftly preach
Eh nearly nivir heard yir nemm
i thi burr o ilka bee;

but ken noo that ut is your breist
eh'm liggin oan tae listen.
Ut is your braith
that blaws thi feathirs o thi wurds
by me and awa.

leese me oan - an expression of preference; lea-laik-gair - the place
where two hills join together and form a kind of bosom; burr - a
whirring noise as made in the throat in pronouncing the letter "r"; liggin
- lying

Halcyon's Comet

Comet, swung awa
intil thi airms o nithin
oan yir silly ellipse,
wi yir hert o slush as snaa
an grime-granita -

Black ice comet,
scrapeit fae thi streets
o Dundee wi a raggity
razir, rowld intae a baa
an skiddin awa -

Sheddin detritus fae
detritus, yi faa
fur nicht, ye hair-
stane hert o haar
an teuch cranreuch -

Weel ye ken
that Eh sall die
afore yi cut ma sky
again, yi cat's claa o a
comet. Sae, guidbye.

hairstane - standing stone; cranreuch - hoarfrost

George Bruce

Rebuke

There was bread left over
at breakfast, a heel of brown bread,
and I broke it and put it on the stone
ledge at the window: and sparrows came,
a blackbird and a black-capped tit,
and it all went quickly.

And the next morning I did the same,
and it went quickly. Then
the bitter wind came and I kept
the window tight-shut, and a sparrow,
one sparrow, sat on a bush by the window
and cursed me in cheeps. So

I put out more bread, and its friends came
and munched and munched and munched,
and the next day the wind blew colder,
and I kept shut the window;
and the cheeping and cheepering went on.
Why should I fear a sparrow's rebuke
when Sarajevo weeps its eyes out?

Repentance

Now I am making a brown parcel
of all my tomorrows, each one a song,
(but of how many I do not know)
to put on the ledge for the cheeping sparrows.

I could guess them, yet still would not know
how to deal with my stained futures.
Sparrows know how to treat
each moment of the day.

In the peek of an eye,
in the flirt of a wing,
in the peck of a beak
in the dust - they know
a meal from a mote.

True Scot

Now at the front door
the candles of the chestnut are lit;
at the back door,
robin, beggar bird of winter.

I hold both in me
at war with myself.

Koala
At Cleland National Park, South Australia

1

Very slowly he moved with sleep
in his drink-sodden eyes
about the trunk. His position
of backside to me, perhaps,
was not intended as insult,
but not, not a camera shot.

Position reversed - cradled
between tree-arm and trunk,
he is looking at me,
so I flatter myself till
I observe the eyes are closed.

Still the relaxed poise suggests,
or allows for, the acceptance
of another's presence,
or was he just bored
with the whole human race?

2

Without a "by your leave" or "may I",
the guide/ presenter of the show
plants the creature on my chest.
The tourists click their cameras,
and "Doesn't he love the dear old man!"

No hint of love or hate, but
indifferently the mammal's claws
are penetrating to my skin.
Am I being signalled that
he and his kin belong
with the dark people
who did not welcome our coming?

In the Train

1

"Are you going to Glasgow?" he said,
as only a man from Glasgow could say.
There was nowhere else for this train to go
so I said nothing, Neither "yes" nor "no",
but stared at the gray man in gray, gray hair,
gray face, his chin and his nose so close,
as if no teeth between, his eyes shut tight,
his lips drawn tight to let nothing get in.
Then as the train sped on its way the light
broke new, spreading its beams on fields
of stubble and green on this November day,
but all I saw was a faceless man,
thin flesh a cover for bones, till Glasgow came.
He opened gray eyes, and bright they shone. "Glasgow!"
he bawled with a laugh that shoved off wrong,
and Sauchiehall Street was one long song.

2

"I come from Shetland."
Time melts as if before acetylene's force.
Eyes open on a micaceous beach,
Tides at a race strand
a whale. Skies high with light;
with birds harsh in chorus strew
the air - talk, talking of gulls,
terns, guillemots, puffins and petrels.
Beneath - the isles assorted in their seas.

Castle Tioram, Loch Moidart

The tide comes in and empties the castle
of all but its bloody memories. The tourists
are gone, the last bustling to the shore
before the tide cut-off, leaving their litter.
Paper bags spin up draughty holes and out,
whisked out to sea. Lords of the Isles
lived here, thinking to themselves – forever.
Gone. What human kind were they anyway?
Pride, courage, cruelty in them, no doubt.
Evening - the loch stills. In its shimmer
Tioram trembles. From the dark cube laughter,
echoes of children, the new invaders -
Andrew, Ken, Karen, Jennifer, Ben -
a play-pen for them. Night,
skraichs - the sea birds have it for themselves.

Mist

Mist shrouds the Firth,
contains all, allows entry
only to the finger
of the mind, contains
time past, hard-backs
resistant to wear of water,
predators predating all
kind, or simples, uni-cellular
expressions, or us mulched to
such fineness as that transparent
air in stratosphere provides.

Moss Agate

As if the North green-weedy sea
had entered in and met the South,
untuous and vinous, suffusing reds
with subtle lights of plum.

And this is stone and common.
No moonstone omen from eternity
but sea-washed, bound for Scotland
when the cosmic pot was on the boil.

Something between the soft, wild lights
of a winter sky and any careless
autumn afterthought, now transfixed,
like Leonardo's famous smile.

Haiku for John Ferguson, Rector of Fraserburgh Academy

Coming home
to the sea-town
shared interests
much understanding

The sun leans
on the low landscape
the sea is kindly
affection stirs

The flat stone
in Kirkton Kirkyard
by the sea's mouth
spells our endless end

The Herbour Wa, MacDuff:
The Fiddle, Banff

for George Gunn

The wa! - the face o blunt rebuttal -
sea's girn, yelloch, yammer, snash, greet
an then thunner that wud smore a - this
the wa took on, whiles the squat beacon licht
signalled hope fae its steen stack tae boats
storm-driven, that, but for it, meth stravaig
heid-on tae wa, an that's an en o't,
an them aboard. Exac timin, steady hauns, keen ee,
tae haud her deid-mid the run o watter tween piers.
The Provider, wi a wecht o haddock, cod, ling, sole,
twa monkfish an a conger we cud duin wioot,
netted saxty mile nor-nor-east Kinnaird,
the nor wun at her stern, heids in atween the gap,
nae a thocht, nae a doot at the rin-in, driven
bi thon hard race. They're for hame, diesel pooer,
as the boats, steam an sail, through a the years.

An up the brae in years lang syne
on the green, green girss o Banff O,
Macpherson jigged an played his spring
aneath the gallows tree O!
It soondit oot sae fresh an free
in caller air that's born at sea,
that's blawn some hame, an mony a one
its blast has taen tae kingdom come.
It soondit oot in sprightly tune
or the cheatin clock stapt fast his rune.
Atook the fiddle in his haunds
an brak its back, syne stiff he stands.
The soul flew oot, the sang's awa,
lost in the cauldrif wun an snaw.
but far ayont the watters mell,
like soon made in a curly shell,
folk hearken yet tae what's nae there,
for them the sang's for evermair.

Betty and Elizabeth at the Piano

Twa auld wives sclim up the stair
their banes creakin as they gang.
In the Georgian drawing room they're
at it. Fower haunds keep time, thrang
in Mozart. A lintie's on the wing.
Keys ring oot as twa lassies gar them sing.

Gorbachov in Stornoway

Donald S. Murray

'How can I, that girl standing there,
My attention fix
On Roman or on Russian
Or on Spanish politics?...

W.B. Yeats, 'Politics'

An extract from the memoirs of Dmitiri Gerenko, Special Adviser to Mikhail Gorbachov, former President of the Soviet Union.

It was Raisa who began our problems that day. Only a few hours before our departure, she made her intentions clear, her high heels sparking as she strutted through the corridors of the Kremlin.

"I will go to Reykjavik." she declared.

The President sighed as he always did when his wife was at her most determined. "Try and dissuade her, Dmitri." he said to me. "Mrs Reagan will not be there. It will not be good diplomacy if she comes along."

I scurried in Raisa's wake as I tried to make her husband's position plain: that this was an important summit meeting, not a PR exercise for the Western media; that Nancy was an important influence on her husband and would not take kindly to her presence; that her very arrival on the plane would be a signal to General Bolgarov and his anti-Western camp that the President was too much under his wife's control to be a man with whom they could do business. But a single haughty look from Raisa was enough to silence all my protests. A couple of hours later and she would be on that plane, her bags packed with the furs and dresses he – privately – deplored, setting off on another expedition to the shops and stores of the decadent West.

And so it turned out to be. Raisa sat behind us as we travelled on the plane that day – the men in the party discussing what weapons we should hoard or surrender in the SALT talks with Reagan over the next few days.

"Do not give too much away." General Bolgarov kept saying, his dark eyebrows as ominous as thunderclouds. "Let us keep as much as we can."

"We need to make some strides towards a lasting peace, Comrade General." Gorbachov explained. "Otherwise our economy..."

It was in the midst of this conversation that the plane began shuddering – its engines trembling as we travelled over the coastline of Norway. Its fjords and cliffs stretched out like fingers threatening to clutch us from our position in the skies.

"There is a fault in our electrics." the pilot declared. "We will do our best to repair it while we are in flight, but we may have to land."

Raisa jibbered in alarm at his words, no doubt foreseeing a moment when the sealskin hat that decorated her head might be restored to its former owners.

"I should have stayed at home." she mumbled in panic. "Mikhail! Why did you ask me to come with you? I should never have listened to you."

Again, that sigh and look of exasperation on the President's face. For a moment, I found myself thinking of all the unhappiness of his domestic life; how he had told me so many times of his longing for the simple peasant women who had cared for him in his childhood, ones without any thought for the furs and perfumes Raisa garnished round her life. "A plain honest-to-goodness woman," he told me one time after he had slipped down a few glasses of vodka. "That's who a man like me would love to meet. But what chance does a man in my position have to do so? So many faces in a crowd. So many seeking power. And in every embrace – even those of my relatives – there may be the kiss of a Judas."

Yet an instant later, the President expelled this unsought pity from my head. He had been listening to the noise of the engine and come to a decision.

"Get the pilot to find an airport where we can land. Nothing must endanger what we are about to do."

I nodded in obedience. Listening to his clipped commands, all thought of Gorbachov the private man vanished and my sense of him as our country's leader was restored.

And that was how we arrived in Stornoway – the plane curling round to land on a flat, treeless island on the north-western edge of Britain. We went down the steps to find our only welcome was a brisk wind that braced and blew. As I drew up my collar to protect my face from its attentions, a memory of my childhood in Tarivostok - a small town in the northeastern part of Siberia – came to mind.

An airport worker dressed in red overalls gaped as a party of Soviet generals and heavy-set men in thick coats and Astrakhan hats marched towards him down the runway. His eyes widened even more as he recognised the President and his wife.

"Where can we wait?" General Bolgarov barked out his question, his military manner never deserting him even in these strange circumstances.

The man pointed towards a little grey building which lay at the edge of the tarmac, dwarfed by the large RAF hangers around it.

"Thank you." he pronounced, leading our delegation through its back door. On one side, there was what probably passed for the Baggage Retrieval Area – a row of steel rollers built at a slant for luggage to roll down. On the other, there was a doorway leading to a small room where coffee and tea could be served. We barged in there, disturbing the terminal's only customers – a number of unshaven men nursing their cold cups of coffee and playing cards. One of them was just placing a trio of aces on the table when we entered, muttering something in his astonishment that was clearly not English.

"Cò bho ghrian...? A Mhafia?"

It was then that Raisa entered. She bustled in behind us, accompanied by her secretary – a thin, leaf-like figure with brown hair and a lime-green suit – and all the time, she was snapping questions, directing them at everyone in her party.

"General Bolgarov..., where did you say we were? ... Oh, and how long did you say we'd be here? ...Is there anywhere we can go while we're waiting? Mikhail, do you think there are any reasonable shops in this place?..."

Even that famous red birthmark seemed to grow pale as he sat down, listening to the words of his wife.

"No..." he said "I don't think this is either the time or the place."

Raisa's brown eyes flashed. "Very well, Comrade President" she declared as she glided over in the card-players' direction. "We will do as you say." A moment or two later, however, we heard the words 'Woolworths' and 'Harris Tweed' emerging from their conversation. The card-players' eyes sparkled as they imagined tips much larger than the sums that ever could be won at an airport poker game.

It was then something happened which I believe changed the whole course of history. A waitress arrived at our table. She had long, black hair, brown eyes and sallow skin – looking for all the world like a senorita washed up on this cold, Northern shore – and a tall, full-breasted form which her shabby red waitress outfit rounded and emphasised. Some thirty years of age, she moved quietly between the tables, placing cups of tea and coffee before the military men and Communist party officials who were her unexpected guests.

Something happened to the President when he saw her. His breath piped down to a whistle. His fingers drummed a tattoo onto the cafe table.

"Look at her." he muttered. "Look at her."

"Yes, Comrade President."

"Her uniform has a hole at the elbow. There is a run in her tights. Can you imagine how Raisa would behave if she was dressed like that?"

My eyes scuttled in the direction of our country's First Lady, wrapped in a swathe of furs and asking for directions to the town's shops. "No, Comrade President."

As she headed in our direction, other aspects of her appearance became clearer. The cuffs of her white sweater were dirty and frayed. Her black skirt was worn and thin. And at the sight of all this – a man who had never blanched before the sparkle of a tiara or the power of a general's insignia – there was a tremor in his voice.

"Coffee or tea?" she asked.

"I-I-I'll h-h-have coffee." he answered, his translator by his side.

The waitress nodded, noting his order on her pad, and moved back to her tiny kitchen at the side of the terminal. The President's eyes haunted her footsteps as she walked across the room, noting her every step and sway; the grace with which she wore her shabby uniform.

And then he seemed to rouse himself from his distraction. He shook his head at his own bemusement and turned to me with a dark and earnest look on his face.

"You know what I would like most in the world, Dmitri? To have a woman like that for my own." He lifted his eyes once again to watch her pouring water from a kettle. "But the world does not permit me such simplicities. Perhaps it will one day."

History records most of what happened after that.

The meeting in that other Icelandic 'White House' where Reagan and the President bargained half the world's weapons away. Where men like General Bolgarov and the executives of defence industries watched and raged in disbelief. Where ordinary people felt for the first time this century that peace might be possible. Where the world media snapped pictures of Raisa as she hurried through Reykjavik's shops and schools, gaining more acclaim and belongings.

Yet there is more to tell than that. There was the morning some months after his replacement by President Yeltsin that Mikhail returned to Stornoway airport. A frail and haunted figure, he dodged through the crowd that had gathered there. A number wore dark suits and Homburg hats; many with stiff white halos that had slipped around their corpulent necks. They were circling around a rather straight-laced young woman who appeared to be wearing sackcloth rather than a dress.

"Yes. He did touch me." she was saying. "I swear he did."

Her words were greeted by a squeal of triumph by one of the men who had assembled there. "We've got him now." he declared. "We've got him now!"

Watching their behaviour, Gorbachov momentarily regretted ever having liberated religion in the Soviet Union, yet he was even more appalled by how much the terminal had changed. A bar was in place where the waitress had once poured her kettle; her replacement a young woman just out of her teens with a tiny metal stud fixed in her right nostril and dark mascara smeared around her eyes. Nevertheless, he went up to her, clutching a piece of paper on which he had written some phrases he had long since learned by heart.

"Where is she? Where is she? Where is the black-haired woman who work here?"

The girl briefly halted her relentless chewing of spearmint to answer his question. "Sorry. Ah dinnae ken whit yer oan aboot."

Baffled, he walked away from her, blending into the group of men wearing the same grey Homburg hats and overcoats as he had on that day. Too busy talking to the woman they had been speaking to earlier, they didn't even appear to notice him when he joined their flight off the island. They were going to their annual Assembly, while he was heading back to Moscow to begin his life again.

Hoover's Housekeeper

Donald S. Murray

'A deep gloom settled over the village of Cairnbost recently when it was discovered that its most celebrated citizen, Miss Nora Jemima Macaulay had passed away at her home in Orange County, California ...'

With these words, the Maransay *Chronicle* announced the death of Nora Jemima – a 'celebrated citizen' whom no-one in the village could remember. There was good reason for this. Ever since the early Twenties when she headed west on the emigré ship, the *Sedna*, she had never returned home. Yet despite her long absence, Nora never suffered the symptoms of amnesia that often affected those exiled a handful of years. From her various homes throughout the States, she kept herself informed of all that was happening in her native village – her knowledge gained by virtue of the fact that, as the Maransay *Chronicle* reported in her obituary "For many years, Nora worked as cook and housekeeper in the home of the former director of the United States' Federal Bureau of Investigation, the late J. Edgar Hoover."

It was not, however, her inquiring mind that gained her this employment. It was, instead, her skills in the kitchen that first drew her to the attention of the young law enforcement officer. In his early years as director, he had taken on a long succession of cooks – each of whom had disappointed him in some way. A plateful of ravioli would, for instance, find him wrinkling his pug-nose in the suspicion that a member of his staff was an agent for the Mafia. A serving of Beef Stroganoff would inform him that his cook was possibly in the pay of the Soviets. Even a helping of Irish stew could be put aside and treated as suspect; maybe this one was in the service of that troublesome Boston Catholic family, the Kennedys.

Into the turmoil of his kitchen came Nora. From the beginning of her time there, the young Hebridean won the trust of her boss. Her servings of herring and potatoes could be chewed over with ease; her porridge swallowed without the thought that it might, somehow, be ideologically suspect. Even in his most paranoid moments, the idea that anyone with dangerous, foreign ideas – like Socialism or Communism – could ever manage to produce a simple joint of mutton never passed through Hoover's head. Instead, he relished her Scotch broth, scones and oatcakes; a smile coming to his thick, heavily-jowled face every evening he anticipated the arrival of her meals.

"My, my, my," he would say as he tucked into yet another of her dinners. "You're a wonderful cook. A lady with amazing culinary skills."

She would shy at his compliments, shrinking into the slight, mouselike girl she always appeared to be in his company. "My mother taught me well." she'd reply.

"She sure did. She sure did." J. Edgar would grin as he rose from the table, setting off to plan yet another arrest in defence of the nation's security. "And I am truly grateful for it."

It was only a matter of time, however, before Nora's other talents were recognised. That moment came one evening when Hoover stepped into the kitchen to prepare a cheese sandwich for himself. Lying beside the bread-bin was a letter Nora was writing to her sister, Marsalli Anne. J. Edgar lifted it in his fingers, reading it with an increasing sense of interest;

'...Is Willie Maclean still drinking? How is his wife putting up with it? Is she still unhappy, still telling her stories to Ishbal Mairi down the road? How on earth does she trust that one? Doesn't she know she's spreading stories all over the place?...'

The more Hoover read, the more he recognised a mind just like his own; the only difference between them was of scale. He smiled at this, marvelling at the thought that an intelligence so perfectly complementing his could be found within the walls of his home.

It was while he stood there reading her letter that she walked in. He noticed her right away, his dark eyes fixing her with the same intense expression that had intimidated so many in the past.

"You're some lady, aren't you?" he grinned.

She said nothing to this, unsure whether to take his words as a compliment or a prelude to being fired.

"I think we can use you." he said. "There's a job where I need someone I can trust..."

Apparently, there was this local politician in Pittsburgh who was deeply involved in a number of graft and corruption cases. He needed someone placed within his household to gather evidence against the man.

"A cook..." he smiled, the broad outline of his body framed in the kitchen doorway. "A cook's the ideal person. After all, the way to any man's trust is through his taste buds."

She laughed at this, agreeing to do as he wanted. In a matter of months, the task was complete; the politician on his way to prison as a result of a conversation she had overheard at his dinner table. Hoover was delighted at her success, the dark, – almost Negroid face which he had spent many hours in his youth attempting to scrub white – beaming as he welcomed her back to his home.

"What can I do for you?" he declared. "How can I reward you for all the help you have given?"

In an instant, Nora knew her answer. For some time, she had been troubled over the reliability of her reports from Cairnbost. She knew too well that Marsalli Anne could hardly be described as an independent witness. She could be concealing information about her own problems; the fact that her husband, John Murchadh Martin drank overmuch; that her children – Lachlann, Nora and Finlay – were plaguing her with troubles. It was the thought of these little gaps in her knowledge that made her make a strange request of Hoover. Would he send a few of his G-men over to Scotland to keep an eye on her fellow-villagers? ... The F.B.I. director smiled in response.

"Is that all you want?"

Nora Jemima nodded.

"Of course, lady. We can easily do that for you."

It was as a result of this agreement that, from the early 1930's onward, strange visitors began to appear in and around the village of Cairnbost. They would turn up on days when the local people were taking home peats for their winter fires, or their fank was full of sheep for the clipping.

Somewhere in their possession would be a notepad, set of binoculars, a camera or two. The villagers would watch in wonder as their every word and movement was observed and noted.

"Towerists!" they would declare contemptuously.

"– Or Hollywood looking for fresh talent!" the young girls would fantasise, putting on their best dresses for a day out on the moor.

But in the files they sent back to Washington, there was much to disturb Nora. Tales of tiny, red-haired John Murchadh Martin and his drunken exploits. How he had deliberately lowered his trousers in front of the American observers and their cameras. (The photographic evidence was enclosed in the file.) How he had declared his support for Communism in a drink-fired argument. How he had composed a love-song in honour of Stalin and Lenin, singing it in the bar of the local hotel. And, worst of all, there was the time he yelled at an inquisitive neighbour.

"You're worse than that creep who's my sister's boss. J. Edgar bloody Hoover!"

Nora read these words in a mixture of terror and dismay. Having a brother-in-law like John Murchadh Martin could easily undermine her position in the Hoover household. Yet there were worse consequences than that. She could imagine mocking voices in the backrooms of the Senate and the White House. "How can we trust a man who offers employment in his own home to those whose relatives are fellow-travellers of the Reds?" She didn't know to know Hoover could manage to answer that question. After all, it was similar to those which he and his fellow G-men had probably asked in a thousand interrogations, using the same words again and again while their suspects sweated under a harsh and glaring light.

The thought of all this troubled Nora for weeks. She made mistakes in her cooking: forgetting to salt the potatoes; letting a pan of milk boil over. There was even one time she broke one of her own cardinal rules and accepted another woman's advice in cooking, adding a dash of paprika to a potful of stew. Hoover's fork paused halfway to his mouth that evening, his eyes following her for a long time before he finally glanced away. It was as if he were starting to suspect her of falling for the harsh ideologies that had overcome much of Europe; the red flare of their flags and emblems tainting even his enjoyment of his evening meal.

It was then she decided to approach him – to tell him of the brother-in-law whose senses had long been subverted by the combined effects of Karl Marx and whisky. She twisted her fingers as she told her story, letting him know that her main concern was the effect it might have on Hoover's own position. The F.B.I. director, however, only smiled grimly when she had finished her tale.

"I'll have a word with Clyde about it," he said, referring to Mr Tolson, his closest colleague in the Bureau. Nora had even seen the two of them dressed in female clothes in her employer's bedroom one morning some months before. 'We're off to a fancy dress party,' Hoover had explained, and she had thought no more about it – apart from the fact it was an odd way of behaving at that time of day.

She stood around, waiting for him to say more, but he never did. Instead, his gaze shifted back to the pile of papers on his desk, the blankness of his expression informing her the interview was over. She went to bed that night still fearful and uncertain, hoping that behind her employer's impassive face, a solution was being considered.

And then, within a month or so, there came an end to her troubles. She read about her brother-in-law's death in a letter from Marsalli Anne. Apparently, a tragic accident had occurred one afternoon then John Murchadh had gone out to gather a few stray sheep from an area of common grazing near the shore. Around four hours later, a search-party left the village to discover where he, too, might have strayed, finding him washed up on some rocks with a half-bottle in his back pocket. 'How many times did I warn him about drinking?' Marsalli asked mournfully in her letter, 'but he never ever listened to me.'

From that day, Nora Jemima was never quite so certain about the world in which she lived. Unsure of the answers she might find to her questions, she chose not to ask any, serving, instead, plates of roast beef he would savour; desserts he might relish; cups of coffee he was able to sip and enjoy. And, of course, in the spare time she had left, she continued to chronicle the life of Cairnbost – her obsession with its activities sending out Federal Agents who would try and blend with the locals chatting at the counter of the village shop, recording their quarrels and disagreements on tape recorders disguised within briefcases, or continuing to post long epistles filled with questions to the home of Marsalli Anne.

As the years went on, the contents of these changed a great deal. Old names disappeared, and new ones – the children of her own generation – took their place. Yet despite this, Nora mailed her letters with the same fervour as before, filing each reply away in huge, dust-covered folios in the housekeeper's quarters in Hoover's home. And when she came to leave there, after Hoover died in the spring of 1972, these went with her, shifting with all her other possessions, to her own house in Orange County. She spent her final days there as the last surviving member of her family – a fact that the Maransay *Chronicle* noted in her obituary, adding that, 'Nevertheless, she still kept in contact with her nieces and nephews on the island. The sympathy of the community is with them at this time, particularly her sister, Marsalli's son, Lachlann who, together with his wife, Lorna, was out visiting his aunt in California at the time of her demise.'

Yet there was more to the end of her life-story than the local correspondent of the Maransay *Chronicle* could ever have imagined. Her death occurred only a week after Lachlann and Lorna arrived on their Hoover free-flight to California (obtained after they had bought a washing machine for their home). They had been met by a small, white-haired lady whose vitality belied the fact she was in her late eighties. Her voice drilled questions incessantly into their ears:

"How's Mairi Maggie? Is she still carrying on with that fellow down the road? Is it true he left his wife behind in Glasgow? Did they have any children? Do they ever...?"

But the splendour of her home soon made up for the discomfort of their arrival. Lachlann stood in awe at the sight of the tigerskin rug in the hallway; his mouth sagged as he stood before her jacuzzi; his eyes could only roll in wonder when he saw a dozen or so sprinklers form a multitude of rainbows on her lawn.

"It's amazing!", he kept saying, "No wonder you never came home."

But later on, there was the night when, looking for a toilet, he stepped into her study by mistake. Switching on the light, he saw the huge folios stacked upon its shelves. 'Cairnbost 1929'; 'Cairnbost 1930'; 'Cairnbost 1931'; the titles on their bindings read. He picked one up – the chronicle for 1934, the year his father died – and turned its pages over.

What happened after that can only be supposition. Did he flick through the papers to discover the photo of John Mhurchadh with his Long Johns at his ankles? Did he scan the FBI agents' reports of his father's actions – the many drunken exploits and remarks noted in the book? Did he discover, too, his mother's letter, informing Nora of her husband's death? And did he, standing there as dawn broke over the western coastline of North America, twist the accounts of these events over and over in his mind till they formed certain hard and definite conclusions? And was his reaction then to turn upon his aunt in a bitter, vengeful rage?...

There are only a few things known for certain about all this.

The following morning, Nora Jemima was found dead at the foot of the stairway in her home. A fortnight later, her obituary in the Maransay *Chronicle* appeared.

Trans-Siberian Days

Chris Harvie

One

"He was almost on me before I could get my gun out. He was taking a swing at me when I shot him in the face." Yuri Pinyagin didn't look the sort of person to be blowing people away. Professors of English don't do this sort of thing, not even to colleagues. Had six months living in Govanhill turned him into the hard man of the Wild East? The gun was a gas-pistol, supposed to choke, not blow brains all over the place. And the problem was vodka, the quickest way out of the City of Perm. "The man pestered me to give him money, and screamed at me in the street till he was crazy. I didn't know it, but he was following me to my house, and then he tried to jump on me." This was during my session with the New Russians, and we were shifting blinis, vodka, caviar, etc in the basement of a bank, guarded by three young men who didn't look very numerate but were toting guns which definately didn't spray tear-gas.

Where is Perm? For a start, it's where Permian sandstone comes from, one of these ancient ascriptions which brand a place, like the luckless Neanderthal in the Ruhr. But much later on it crops up as Varikino, in *Dr Zhivago*, where Zhivago finds his Lara in the midst of the Russian Civil War. The house in which Pasternak placed the action has gone, but another, looking just as time-worn, stands in its place, where equally lived-in trams rattle over a crossing guaranteed to eviscerate any car that takes it at more than five miles an hour. Downhill, long rail and road bridges cross the River Kama, and trains six days out from Vladivostok begin their last twenty-four hours to Moscow. The place - then called Molotov after Stalin's charmless but resilient henchman - really started to expand when production was evacuated to it during the German invasion. 1.2 million Permians now live along fifty miles of the banks of the Kama, which is rather like imagining a city stretching from Stirling to North Berwick, making guns, aero engines and at the Felix Dzerzhinski Factory chain-saws (how else would you commemorate the founder of the Cheka?)

I am there to talk about "Philosophy in Scottish Literature" (a threateningly MacDiarmid-like project) to the Russian English Teachers' Conference. Handled like a parcel on every stage of my trip from Berlin by Volodya, Sasha, Natasha, *et al*, careful to see that I got out of the hell which is Moscow's Sherementevo airport, I rolled into Perm after a full day on the Baikal Express, trundling at thirty-five miles an hour over the great Russian plain. This sounds horrendous but was a sort of object-lesson in generosity and coexistence, with total strangers offering, rather peremptorily - "Eat please!" - masses of food and drink and not minding at all if you just curled up and fell asleep. Outside an unending vista of wood and moor unrolled, punctuated by *one* hill, about 200 feet high, and more often by decaying timber-yards and cement works, left lying around in a sort of cosmic untidiness. Every so often we roared over echoing girders, and there was a river and barges, an onion tower, allotments and *dachas*, and long platforms where grannies sold beer and rolls out of Claudia Schiffer plastic bags, in a canyon of shabby green trains.

Two

Perm loomed up in the drizzle of evening, and the sound of "the Slavic Women's March" (a rowdy lot, evidently), and a posse was waiting on the platform with the one car they could commandeer. An hour later I was munching my way through a mountain of *piroschki* - a sort of pancake-clad bridie - with Liana, Sacha and Dasha, who at fourteen was into English (which his mother teaches) and computers, and regarded my stone-age Sanyo as a throwback as remote as the Hillman Imp.

The conference, held in half-a-dozen gey dreich halls, turned out to be magic, with charming girls whispering translations of papers - on Stevenson, Auden, Yeats - whose breadth and originality broke out of the frozen categories of the past, far different from the opaque *theorie* which would, sure as fate, confront me at, next stop, the German *Anglistentag* in Greifswald. I did my stuff as one of the keynote speakers, and ended up fleetingly on television - a change from endless game shows, American crime movies, and Vladimir Zhirnovsky thumping people in the Duma. Philosophy and the novel was the theme of the conference, and I covered the Scottish common-sense school and its influence, from Henry MacKenzie and Scott, via George Davie, to Gray and Kelman, doing my bit for the Adam Smith of "sympathy" rather than the caricature of the man as a demon of self-interest peddled by the toxic economists - including a few members of the famous Forsyth Menagerie - parachuted in by the West since 1990. See below for their finest achievement.

"But you haven't mentioned Lewis Grassic Gibbon!" This comes up in the question session. The man/men from the Mearns has/have seemingly a lot of fans in the Urals; a lot less was known about MacDiarmid, who can't have visited the place. (When he did, as in Budapest, folk remember, indelibly). Only a few miles past the tram terminal you could be out of the world and into pine-fringed upland and villages of dark-timbered houses where nothing much seemed to have changed for a century, where there lurks, presumably, that Great Green International ... There's also much interest in Stevenson and Hogg, raising other, less optimistic notions of dualism and fractured identity. Psychiatry was notoriously unpopular under the old order, save as an excuse for shoving dissenters into asylums. But one senses that having had in recent years to deal with two virtually separate Adam Smiths, a cooler view of liberalism will have few illusions about its unalloyed benefits.

Three

Boris Proskurnin, who is head of the department of World Literature at the University, had managed to persuade the country's English scholars out of Moscow, no mean feat as Perm is probably the place where Chekhov's three sisters moaned about being hundreds of miles away from the capital. He lodged here for a few weeks in the 1890s, en route to Sakhalin, and we had sessions in a little theatre he must have known, built by the governor's wife in the Summer Residence. At Perm one senses not distance but the importance of intersection - where the land route crosses the water-route. The Trans-Siberian got here in 1892, but long before then the place was a great inland port. Sergei Diaghilev was born in 1872 in a big pink merchant's house on the edge of the Old Town; Maxim Gorki, four years older, saw the place from a different angle, as a cook on one of the river steamers which still supply the place with fruit and vegetables from the Caspian and the tropical south. Not to speak of Stroganoff, of Boeuf fame, who founded the place in 1723, using timber from the huge Ural forest, brought down by rafts on the Kama, to smelt local copper ore and purify salt. A ridge of buff-and-cream Tsarist terraces fronts the Kama, half-a-mile wide, with ships coming upstream which are proper coasters, not barges. From here it's possible, via the Caspian Sea and the Volga-Don canal, to navigate to the Danube and the Rhine.

Perm is an anthology of New and several Old Russias. Yuri and his banker friend Dmitri - "another old Comsomol man" seem rather like Gordon Brown and Tony Blair learning capitalism while keeping bits of "this great movement of ours" around for sentiment's sake. There's still a Lenin Street and a Soviet Boulevard, with the great man fronting the Opera House and shaking hands with Gorki at the University. At the same time the art gallery is being converted back into the cathedral which it once was. All the social realist work seemed to have disappeared from the collection, and been replaced either by boring modern abstracts or icons. A few icons go a long way, especially if they're modern and show the wonder-working qualities of Tsar Nicholas II.

Russian meals are elaborate, the vegetables and pickles excellent - "we survived on our pickles in the awful winter of '91-92" - and instead of the dreaded vodka toasts, there is beer from the Viking Brewery which some wandering German started a century ago, and succulent water-melons from Astrakhan. Dinner at the bank offers caviar and blinis and the only vodka I drink, otherwise shifting a decent supermaket wine from the Rhineland which is reckoned a luxury. I take my New Russians – Yuri the professor and Dmitri the banker – at their word, because neither looks as if he's rolling in it, without so much as a Lada between them, dependent for getting around on the crammed buses and trams. New Russians are to be found in the universities, as law and economics are the big growth areas, and after them English. But the big money isn't in education, even less so in manufacturing, but in import-export.

"How many New Russians succeed?"

"About one in three. You need connections; if you haven't got them, and you're up against the Mafia, you haven't much chance."

Neither has any intention of clearing off from this shambolic but friendly place. To them the Mafia is real, as are the hopeless drunks wanting to try things on in the streets. But there's the chance of getting some kind of civic society going, and something in the easy familiarity and hospitality of people on the train, in the university, or in tiny methodically-run flats, which encourages you to hope.

Four

Back in Moscow Irina, a professor at the university, said that she'd originally supported Gorbachev, and shifted to "wild capitalism" after the 1991 coup, when it seemed that he was going to compromise with the old guard. She now thought, however, that some sort of social democracy was necessary, and would have voted for Gorbachev had he stood against Yeltsin for the presidency. This seemed a fairly typical learning curve within the new democracy, but it didn't help Gorbachev much.

Perm averaged out, I suppose, at more or less where Gorbachov wanted Russia to be, but the compromise is a spiky one. The big state-run industries survive, with slimmed-down workforces, desperately searching for markets. The new economy bases itself on supplying the Permians with food (good, as although what was available under the old order was cheap, you had to queue all day to get it), and electronic goodies (hmmm ... electronic gadgetry flown in from the United Arab Emirates is fostering a television landscape as dire as the USA). The handing-over of houses to sitting tenants curbed the worst of hyperinflation for most people; so far the greater freedoms available compensate for the tiny salaries of the professionals. The New Russians are on probation, and – if Dmitri the banker is anything to go by – reckon that they stand or fall with the city. Indeed, the distance from the centre of power in Moscow seems to have produced a consensus among Duma members of all parties that a more powerful level of regional democracy is necessary, which would take over the planning and welfare powers which were traditionally vested in the big industries.

Where to start? The place is littered with huge mastodons of Soviet architecture, though Stalinist flats are handsome externally, and inside, if they're small, there also well-insulated and rather comfortable. As in Scotland, the real horrors were the system-built flat blocks of the 1960s and 1970s. Like so much else in the East, the private sphere functioned while the public sphere was only fitfully effective. The cinema, circus and ballet (Perm regards itself as Russia's equivalent of Stuttgart as a ballet centre) were still going great guns, while public sanitation looked as if it had been installed by Ivan the Terrible and then forgotten about. The Old Town with its elaborate wooden houses, built with carved, fake-stone, ornamentation, was decaying into near-jungle and the later Jugendstil quarter wasn't far behind.

The Permians and their schools, sewage, trams, and three universities need money and organisation but, more importantly, they need interest from abroad. Thanks substantially to personal contacts, and in particular the role of Karen Hewitt of Kellogg College, Oxford's extra-mural centre, they are getting a lot of help from Oxford, an example of town-twinning that seems to be yielding dividends. But this is the sort of place – and it's broadly typical of many Russian provincial cities – where boxes of books, old but reliable computers, subscriptions to journals, visiting lecturers, go a very long way. The more you see of Perm's problems, but also of the human resources raring to be mobilised, the more you see the importance of building up tri-lateral systems of co-operation – particularly between Britain and Germany – which can deliver a blend of technical and cultural co-operation. To return to Greifswald, almost indistinguishable from a West German town after only four years, and encounter a couple of hundred German professors solemnly conferring forever and ever amen, was to see both the advantages and the formidable drawbacks of *Vorsprung durch Technik* as an export article, even leaving aside 1941-45. But add *gemeinschaft*, community, the music of things happening?

Five

New Russia has reached us via images of Thatcherite hitmen, drunks and nationalist psychopaths. Trying to leave Moscow promised the worst. Schermetevo was clogged with huddled masses clutching huge suitcases, filing with geological slowness past Sharon and Tracy doing their nails in customs. The hours to the Berlin departure were dwindling into minutes. According to Karen H. the magic formula was just to persist, so I swooped on the nearest unengaged Sharon and shouted that I had to get through or I would miss my plane.

"Nyet!"

Persist!

"The Berlin flight is leaving in twenty minutes and I'll miss it!"

"Moment."

Then a small official popped round a counter, stamped everything in sight and motioned me through, case unexamined and notionally packed with guns, dope, freeze-dried plutonium and what have you.

Reportage tends to come from the centre or crisis areas like Chechenya, and some of the most horrific statistics scarcely get noted at all: for instance, that the West has invested $ 2.5 billion in Russia, but Russian "wild capitalists" have at the same time smuggled $ 40 billion abroad. Contacts whose business connections have taken them to Moscow convey a pretty depressing spectacle of an order combining all the worst aspects of capitalism and Stalinism. These exist, but in the provinces the folk are "most remarkable like us": decent, generous, and fun to be with. They need support, but they repay it many times over.

Dance to Your Daddy

Bernadette Maria Creechan

"Och, they're ... they're ... em I'm keeping them for a good thing, angel"

1 ... 2 ... 3 ... bite my tongue ... 4 ...5 ....

"Surely you don't need a man in your life before you can indulge in the ultimate luxury of wearing nice underwear."

Hand slaps down on my cheek. Won't cry. Won't –

I run upstairs and, kicking the door shut, fall on the bed. Need to get a breath. Where's my inhaler? Aaaah. For crying out loud man, I was only stating a fact.

Cramps tug at my womb. I bite the pillow, and listen for footsteps on the stairs. Bloody hell. It was only some nice knickers, an innocent bra and a trial-size tube of hair-removing cream I got free with the groceries at the store. No-one's asking her to go to a health farm in Beverley Hills. And plastic surgeon in Hollywood.

Happy Birthday.

I feel her crying. Her and her nervous tendencies. Having cardiac arrests every time I say the bloody word. You know, I once said, "Man I'm dying for a shit". She flipped.

I must have bought her what – at least half a dozen sets of silky under-wear, a couple of neat bikinis, and what – say three vouchers for the sauna in town. All this on a good paper round after school and a few hours in the store on Saturdays too.

If there's anything I can't stand it's people not using presents someone has gone out of their way to buy for them. I mean, alright, we've all had the Jumper Out Of Hell from Senile Auntie Flo, but there are times in life when you've just got to shut your face and smile through gritted teeth. (Oh – Auntie Flo is the only relative we ever visit.) She stinks of piss and rouge, and she's at least a hundred and fifty. She's blind, deaf and on another planet. You know, it takes three bus journeys, a ferry and a taxi just to get there. Thing is, you could be a piece of talking shit for all she knows, because she doesn't seem to know we're there half the time. I'd rather die than go, but I learned to stop protesting ages ago. And it's always the same monotonous routine. Give her the sweeties (She doesn't even share them, which may be one consolation for going), then hold your breath as the slimy kiss sucks off your face and your lunch does ten somersaults and a hairy fit in your belly. She doesn't say much, only twitters at intervals. Like a crow. A dying one. And the saliva. Spilling like a string of pearls onto her pink jumper. It's funny you know, when she does talk. She calls

Ma "George". Ma says dementia does that to you.

Anyway, Ma right, she loves perfumes, and getting her hair done up all fancy. She really looks the business sometimes. With her hair all twirly bits and – (Well her wig – she suffers from premature al-o-peesh-a, it runs in her –) God, that spider up there's really bugging my brains.

I don't know. Maybe I shouldn't be the one buying Ma nice things. But I don't mind. Under the circumstances.

His name's on the card. Hey, maybe that's what did it. Shit. I never thought of that.

Like Hell's Bells her sobs rise. Enough to waken the dead. And murder the living. I pull a pillow over my ears and kick the bed hard. Oh no – check me out in that mirror. Think I'll let my hair down – it looks kinda skimpy like this. I love my hair. It's full and thick and silky and I can wear it up or down or – hey s'getting mighty dull out there.

I open the jewel box. It's playing my song. *Our* song. We used to dance to it, me stood on his feet, mad. We called the figurines after ourselves. That's me - the one with the rosy cheeks and the big fancy frock. Over and over. Over and over he would wind up the box and we'd go gliding over the floor as grand as any King and Queen.

Ma cries every time she hears it. I wind it up again.

A crazy image flashes into my mind – any kids I ever have (fat chance with her around – I can hardly mention a guy's name – even from a pop group – or she goes mad, says you shouldn't get too close to people, they try to get right into your business, into your life) – oh yes, the kids, baldy at five right, with false teeth and hobbing to school on zimmers. I laugh, almost choke, as the red handprint begins to fade to tingling pink on my cheek.

These pills are so vile. 1 ... 2 ... 3 ... Right, here goes. Whooh. I don't know what's worse the taste or the tiny blades that stab at my spine. Nasty bastards. S'not as if I can draw any sympathy from her. See, she never seems to know what to say when it's my "time". You know I tried to broach the subject once and, after a few stuttering outbursts, she left the room. To "wash the dishes". I'd already washed the dishes. I felt sorry for her, in a – I don't know – a strange sort of way. I started putting extra boxes of Tampax in with the groceries.

Hey, maybe it's not natural. Maybe it's taboo. Like a lot of things in our house. Like the subject of his grave.

I hate this bit. The "just-eaten-a-chalk-factory" taste. Not long until I hit Jellypark mind you. I like that bit. Give it a rap down there, eh. That's the "poor-me-my-daughter's-a-nasty-wee-bitch" one. Hmmm. Wonder if I should go down and say sorry. I could murder a chip butty and some coke. Hell, this always happens. Bloody drama queen. I'm sat up here feeling guilty for something she started.

The Menopause. Now that's what it could be. I read about it in a magazine. Mood swings? Yes. Nervy? Yes. Flying off the handle when someone commits the crime – of buying you a birthday present? YES! Everything I say is wrong these days. We hardly ever have a laugh any more and going for a pizza is right out the window. Ever since I told her I've contacted the Cemeteries Department. I think the pain of losing him has made her block out where his grave is. I can't wait to surprise her. Flowers. We could take flowers. He'd like that. I guess she must be nervous about it all. But why does she have to take it out on me? I'm doing my best to help.

Well, hey, check out that sky. Sun's gone down. Clouds roll violently. Like the anger on her greying brow. I light the fire. That's better. Wow! Here it comes. Rumbling hard. Like my belly. I love being up here when it's so angry out. Aah. Beautiful.

She hates thunderstorms.

Like a TV screen switched on and off, his framed face is illuminated on the window ledge. Mustn't catch eyes with him. Hurts too much. Too ... too ... no, got to count to ten, control it. The gifts. The slap. This ... empty room. Cold and empty.

Everything that ever bugged me about her is beginning to amplify in my head. Stop it now. 1 . . . 2 . . . 3 . . . . Every fart she ever did reverberates like an earthquake in my ears.

Daddy. Where are you? Here, take my quilt. Stay out of the storm. Stay safe Daddy.

Blood oozes from my arm. I have to do this. She makes me.

Yellow ice-cream is smeared over my chubby sunburnt face, a sandy bucket sits lopsided on my head. Up on Daddy's shoulders I'm perched, my chin on his head, my hands clasped over his eyes. The perfect family shot. Like a photographic development ad. All sun, sand, sea and family fun. Daddy wears flip-flops and Ma's bikini top for a laugh. Ma isn't in the photo.

Clutching the picture, I lie back and hold it to my heart. It's the only one I've got. *We've* got, rather. Ma says Granny McEvoy in Ireland's got all the family shots. So she can be close to us.

Check out that rain man. Very impressive. Very loud. Blood drips thickly from my arm. I suck it hard.

Aooow! What a fuck of an almighty cramp. Suddenly I find myself in the foetal position. 1 ... 2 ... 3 ... got to count to ten. Bite photo hard. Deep breath. Close eyes. His voice tells me everything will be alright.

In Ma's voice. In fucking Ma's voice. Stop it! Go away! Want to hear his voice. Daddy. Talk to me. Please. Why does she keep sneaking in Daddy, why does she keep sneaking in with her voice? Huh. Won't even let me have a minute with my own father. Go away, Ma's voice! Go away!

Somebody hold me. Pamper me. Bring me a water bottle and warm tea. Tuck me in all cosy.

Big Da George would have tucked me in. He used to tickle me on his lap. On the big red chair. And tell me stories. Fantastic stories.

She hardly touches me anymore. Except on special occasions. Like five minutes ago.

I ran up to her once right, and bounded on to her lap, pleading for a bedtime story. As my hand landed on the jelly lump under her belly, she shrunk away from me, pushing me onto the floor. It must have been -

ssshh – The Big C. We did tumours in science. They're dead common.

This is a nightmare. But I won't make the first move. I'd sooner starve to death.

Check out that ceiling. What a disaster. There's magic paint left over from the mural we did in the spare room too. You should see it. Ma's pretty good at art. She did most of the outlining. I did the colours. But every time I suggest doing the ceiling, it's "Not right now, dear". Huh. "In case we move again".

Know what really gets me right. If I ever go into her room without knocking first, she turns into an orbit case struck by 1000 volts of electricity. She grabbed me once right, when I came to tell her the Avon lady was calling, and smacked me till my backside was numb. Just because she was in the nude.

I saw her breasts. They were tiny. I think she believes, or wants to believe, that I won't remember this. S'funny, they always look quite, well, like breasts, when she's dressed. She cried after she hit me, smothered me with kisses till I almost turned blue. My arse throbbed to the rhythm of her sobs, as she pulled me tight to her flat bosom. They hurt like hell those sobs. They really did. Then she took me to see a Bette Davis film. She loves Bette Davis. That's where they met. Ma and Daddy. On a rainy afternoon downtown. So guess you could say that Bette Davis played Cupid. She has also been a psychiatrist for my Ma.

Drowsiness. Rumbling belly. Thunder. Sobbing. Red-hot wedge tries to prise open my arse. I hang upside down and inside out from Mars.

I can remember my first period dead clear. I was six. There's this tree swing up the lane from ours right. Anyway I slip off it one day, go flying through the air, and crash into a pile of bottles. My arse bursts wide open and the world falls out. I scream blue murder as my white hotpants become rapid damp red. Suddenly Mr Johnson from next door's running up to ours with me in his arms, pushing aside a sea of snottery kids whose white faces float around me like ghostly balloons, their stunned expressions rendering me already dead and buried.

Sssh. I think the noise has stopped. She must have cried herself to sleep. Might get a chip butty yet.

Nee-naw-nee-naw-neee – Ambulance. Mr Johnson. Stairs. Ten at a time. Door. Bursts open. Ma. Drunk? Blood. Me. Arse. Throb. Throb. Ma. Face. Horror. Pain. Knife. Floor. Heap. Clothes. Ma. Sob. Blood. I hit the floor like a ton of bricks. Last thing I remember is my red shadow spilling over the cream carpet.

After that, the other kids stopped playing with me. There was gossip I think. But so what – my Ma was naked in the privacy of her own home. If Sam Johnson had a problem with that, he did have a fucking problem. And if my Ma had a really bad period – well, that's nature. Anyway, given the circumstances, with my life and my arse at stake, Ma's nudity was surely trivial.

Ma's right. People are strange.

So suddenly I was the Kid That Nobody Played With. And suddenly poor Ma was the neighbourhood's "Twisted Perv". Some people are sick.

Suits. Two suits. Black? I'll never forget that chap on the door. And the look on Ma's poor face. We had to play "Hide and Sleep" then. Or they might "take me away". "I love you", she kept saying, over and over, tears choking her. I managed to hold my breath for ages. Till my leg died. Then Ma covered my mouth, gently to stifle my scream. I did "brilliant".

I think it was pretty soon after, that we moved out of town. Again. Another new school. Not fitting in with the other kids. Ma always managing to protect me from the world.

See that candle, the blue one, Ma doesn't like it. I use it to pray to Big Da George. I once caught her trying to pretend it'd fallen into the basket by accident. Blue isn't her best colour.

Bang! Hey what is this man – Born in a Park Week or what? Is that supposed to make me feel guilty? I can't believe she's going out. Probably to show me how tough she is. Look at her struggling against the rain, headed for the pier. What's she like?

"Never pass up on an opportunity". That's what she used to say to me all the time. Well some opportunities can't wait.

I pick up the phone and begin to dial, keeping one eye on the window.

This is mad. Phoning a cemeteries department. Do people – alive people – actually work in places like this? A shiver runs through me, as the surprisingly pleasant voice takes my message and leaves me holding. Jingle Jangle, recorded tune, Jingle Jangle –

What? Some kind of confusion? Well, is Mickey Mouse there then? What do you mean you can't fucking find it?

Blood. Heap. Stab. Gossip. Stab. Move. Blood. Suits. Hide-and-Sleep. Run away. Got to run away. Keep ... running

Can't reach wall. Dizzy. Inhaler, where's my in–

Falling. Falling. Spinning. The jewel box catches my arm. It crashes to the floor. Daddy Dancer's head snaps off, and rolls towards me, stopping in the middle of the me Dancer's frilly skirt.

Lights go out in my head. Where's my fucking inhaler? The head rocks before me, bouncing off the wall determinedly, trapped like a wild beast in a frilly skirt. The face slows down, Laughing at me, laughing ... laughing ... laugh ....

Owen Gallagher

A Common History

Here in "Little India", Southall,
beliefs run as deep as the Ganges.
Events abroad can cause a flood at home.

In our classroom, infants are steered in,
tongues paddling away in Punjabi, Hindi,
Gujerati. English is my only tongue.

Thoughts and flags are raised like sails.
The children's minds are filled with cargo,
hauled through choppy seas.

At home time, mums appear in saris,
pilot them back into their mother tongues.
Sprinkle palms with Indian sweets.

Their children are pulled by currents
between banghra and pop, salwars and levis,
black or white skins.

Some will drift to eastern shores, a few
will buy titles from the Crown, become Lords
and Ladies, most seek a common ground.

Here, I'm an outsider. I've lost
my Gaelic tongue. My past flows back to
"Little Ireland", Gorbals, where I ran from.

Mother

She was the pillar of the house,
forever on her knees, straightening
our lives out like tablecloths,
attending mass religiously.

In and out of pawnshops
and washing lines she'd weave,
dosed on tranquillisers
and Electro-Therapy.

Dusting the frills in other homes
to keep our name on the door,
she'd nurtured the thought of being a nun
but found herself in a pinafore.

Seasons rarely changed her days
as she scrubbed and polished each pew.
When we came to lay the stone on her grave,
she'd our names inscribed on it too.

God The Father

Each night he came home, he brought in a silence,
that filled our throats like concrete.
We sat mute at the table, saying Grace
before and after to ourselves.

He would retire to the fire behind a layer of paper,
using pictures as clues,
whilst we recited the rosary
for everyone but us.

Night shuttering us in,
he would climb into the kitchen bed,
us bedded between them like cement,
tiny reproductions of themselves.

Sister Norah's Story

Her tongue was like a catapult,
throwing back words, phrases, promises
I'd made, pelting me with guilt,
until her anger toppled
into the garden of flesh.
Two Eves wrapped like vines
round each other.

As she slept I untwined myself,
to fulfil a vow,
become Christ's bride.
Here in the nunnery
I wear a halo on my finger,
his band of gold. My groom is mute
so I commute within myself.

My days are spent sifting
the lives of female saints,
from Afra the prostitute,
to Veronica, woman of pity,
rewriting their hagiographies,
undoing the male
hand on history.

A swarm of bees nightly
in the hive of my head.
How I long for chocolates
and novels after prayer.
Instead I draft letters
and poems, burn wax
until I tire of myself.

The Trouble With Willie

David Mackenzie

The trouble with Willie is that he doesn't know what his troubles are. No, that's not true; he knows, but he refuses to name them. *Name them,* I tell him, *it's the beginning of control.* He gives me that odd look then. He leans across the table, spreading ash from his roll-up on the scuffed surface between us, and asks me, *What's the time?*

The trouble with Willie is that he's too small. That isn't quite true either. His trouble is that he's a drunk and he's too small. He gets into fights which he loses. People he has never met before beat him up and take his money; people he has known for years beat him up and take his money. Willie often has money, but only for very short periods of time.

Willie drinks too much, has no home, no (legal) income. He's small, ugly and very dirty. He smells. He spits in the faces of old ladies and steals their handbags. He takes out his cock in public and waves it at people. These are his troubles and this is perhaps his main one: he is very, very, very difficult to like. But he is here, now, sitting in front of me, the smell of him, old wine, puke and urine, drifting across to me as he scrabbles about on the table top to retrieve the roll-up that has slipped from his fingers. He is almost sober and has begun to cry. Right now I'm thinking that maybe he'll tell me, now, he'll make a start. Now. But he just says, *What's the time?*

St. Martin's 10 till 4 weekdays, soup kitchen at 8 at weekends; Seymour Place 9.30 to 4, closed weekends; St. Botolph's 2 to 4 every day; The Crypt 9 to 3.30. The Colony, The Open Door, The Sally Ann, The Refuge, St. Michael's; 9 to 3, 9 to 2.30, 2 to 4, 1.30 to 6, 10 till 2.

He wipes his face with a handkerchief that is dirtier than his dirty face. He looks at me and says, *You know what my trouble is?* I lean forward. *Tell me, Willie,* I say. *Tell me. I've lost my watch,* he says.

Visits

Laureen Johnson

It was a normal visit to Agnes. Normally dull, normally demanding and, as usual, hastily pushed to the far back of the mind as soon as doors and distance would allow.

"Mam, does doo no ken wha dis is?"

"No I."

"Mam! It's Christine, dee graand-daughter. Wir aaldest lass. Doo surely kens Christine. Christine, spaek tae her."

"Weel, Granny, foo are you?"

The brown eyes, so vague, remained unrecognising. No flicker of affection. No light of life, no point, then, in telling her about the baby. Then the inevitable. "Weel bairns, since you're come, will you tak a cup o tay?"

They murmured the usual, "Na, na, you never need budder."

"My mercy," Agnes rose on slippered feet. "You're no comin in ta me an no gettin a cup o tay. You're laekly fantin." She headed for the door.

They had long since learned to time their visits to the hospital tea trolley. The understanding nursing staff gently played the routine, providing cups, tea and a plate of biscuits, which Agnes was allowed to press upon her visitors to her heart's content. She saw them off at the door of the ward, issuing warm invitations to come along again. She would never remember she had seen them. On the way out, they met Davie of Leagarth.

"Foo is dee midder, Babs? Just da sam?"

"No just sae ill da day. She kent me."

"Poor Agnes. She wis aye dat fine ta come in tae."

Two years ago, fresh out of college, Christine had asked questions. The answers were always the same. Agnes was in a fairly advanced state of senile dementia. She was physically quite well, she appeared to be happy enough, she was always busying herself about. That was it.

At first, Christine could hardly bear to leave at the end of visits; then, she could hardly bear to visit at all. Now she had reached a stage of acceptance where visits were routine, difficult at the time but not allowed to haunt you. Necessary. Something you endured because it was your duty. That was the message her mother always seemed to convey. Babs had always been strong on duty. Christine could quote her, chapter and verse.

"Someen wid need ta geng." "You hae ta help your neebor." "It's only right. It's wir place ta be dere."

Babs' sense of duty had suffered greatly at the time of Agnes' admission to hospital. She had looked after her faithfully until a difficult situation had become openly dangerous. Time had ceased to mean anything to Agnes. She rose and wandered the house at all hours. She was no longer safe with boiling kettles or electricity.

For months Babs had explained, would still explain: "Geordie said..." – "I didna laek ta do it, but..." – "She nearly set da hoose on fire." – "Da doctor cam an telled wis it wis da best thing." Poor Mam. Always feeling responsible. Always feeling guilty.

The visit over, shopping was a pleasure. Well through the afternoon, they came back to Babs' house, chatting gaily as they carried in groceries, bringing up short at the sight of a jacket slung over the foot of the stairs. Martin was home. The boat must be ashore early.

"Well, sister?' came the slightly slurred voice from the living-room sofa. 'Done dee duty for dis week?"

"Yes," said Christine crisply. "Mair as doo can say."

He needed a shave.

"How can Mam pit up wi dee?" she demanded, standing over him in disgust. "Doo's a bloody disgrace, lyin aroond full o drink in da efternune."

He sat up, beer can in hand. "I am not drunk. I'm no sleepit in thirty-two hoors, dat's aa."

"Huh! Foo mony times are we heard dat een?"

Babs rushed to pacify them. Nothing upset her so much as a family row. "Bairns, bairns, paēce wi you! Martin, is doo needin onything ta aet?"

"No thanks, Mam. I hed in Lerook."

"Dat wid a been hoors ago! I'll mak dee something."

"Doo needna budder." The voice was expressionless. "I'm no hungry."

"Weel, I tink I'll mak wis aa a cup a tay."

"Mak ta you twa if doo laeks." Martin was abrupt. "I'm no wantin!"

Babs was hesitant at the kitchen door.

"Come on, Mam." Christine decided for her. "I'll help dee pit awa dis errans. Never leet wi tay." She drew her mother into the kitchen and closed the door.

There followed a few minutes of Martin talk and Martin concern, the usual stuff you heard every week from Babs. Christine refrained from telling her yet again that she was too soft with him, and fussed over him too much. She changed the subject deftly back to her forthcoming baby, still a novelty to talk about. When she left for home, the mood was again warm and pleasant, and Martin, now heavily asleep on the sofa, did nothing this time to spoil it.

Jim was on back shift at Sullom Voe, and would not be home till late. Christine ate alone, sparingly and healthily. About half past ten she was unpleasantly surprised by a visit from Martin. The door flew open and there he stood, very far from sober. Probably on his way from the pub.

"Doo'll excuse me clutterin up dy boannie hoose," he said, "but da cops is sittin at da loch." He lurched to a chair and sat down heavily. Christine's heart sank. He might stay for hours.

"I can gie dee a run hame," she said, rising from her seat.

He eyed her unsteadily, yet his gaze was penetrating. "Canna suffer me ta sit? Canna bear ta hae a drunk aroond da place? Might mak it look untidy?"

She turned away to hide the blush, and took a deep breath. "Sit still," she said, with as much calm as she could muster.

"What grace!" said her brother. "What hospitality! What a blydely body ta come in tae!"

She should not let herself be riled. But there was no remark, however innocent, which would not arouse a stinging reply. Martin was in that kind of mood. "I'll get dee a cup a tay," she said, and sought refuge in the kitchen. To her dismay, he followed.

"Very good, Chris," he said, making a great show of looking at his watch. "I'm been in da door two meenits an ten seconds an doo's makkin tay. Is doo tryin ta brak Mam's record?"

"Oh very funny, Martin. Geng an set dee doon!"

He ignored her and leaned against the kitchen units. "Family tradition. Thirty meenits athoot maet, mak tay. Veesitors approachin, mak tay. When in doubt, mak tay. My midder's philosophy o life."

"My God!" Christine rounded on him, unable to restrain herself. "Don't doo mak a fool o Mam! She does a damned sight ower muckle for dee!"

"I don't ax her tae!" He glared at her. "An doo's da wan ta spaek, leddy muck!"

Eyes wide, she cried, "What does doo mean?"

"I come home as little as possible," he said fiercely. "If I hed onywye else ta go, believe me, I wid go! I canna stop her feedin me, an fussin ower me. I ax for nothing! An dee? Da dutiful daughter? Doo's goin ta go swannin back ta wark after twartree mont, isn' doo, an laeve Mam ta look after dee bairn for dee? *Aa* day, *every* day! Now *dat's* something ta ax!"

"I *did*na ax! She wanted ta do it, redder as me ax onybody else..."

"Huh!" He laughed shortly and scornfully. "She wanted ta do it! Whan did wir midder ever do onything she *wanted* ta do?"

"What ta hell is doo spaekin aboot? Doo's daft!"

"Chris, doo kens damned fine what I mean! Mam does things at she *haes* ta do, things at she wid *need* ta do, things at she feels she *ought* ta do. Can doo ever in dy whole life mind her doin wan thing just for da sheer enjoyment o doin it - just ta plaise hersell?"

Eyes. Challenge. And fury, sheer fury. Answer. Answer. Answer?

"Martin, doo's exaggeratin! Doo's spaekin dirt! Mam wis aye cheery. Still is – when she gets da chance."

"Der a certain satisfaction," said her brother, in a quieter, bitter tone, "in doin your duty – I suppose." The boiling kettle snapped into silence. Christine, reaching automatically for the teapot, found her hands were shaking. Martin, unexpectedly, drew out a chair.

"Set dee doon, Chris. I soodna a bawled at dee. Doo's delicate." He took the teapot from her and made the tea.

She looked up at the strangely softened face, waiting for the next barbed comment. None came. Curiously, his sudden gentleness was more disturbing than his anger. She thought she might cry. "What wis Mam sayin aboot me?" she asked hesitantly.

"Very little. She just explained ta me an Dad at taytime how doo couldna afford ta stop wirkin, even though doo might laek tae, because o da mortgage problem. An how Jim towt at his job wisna dat secure. I assume dat's what doo telled her?"

"Yes, I *did* tell her dat, but ... weel, Jim's job'll lest for a start yet. An it *wid* be hard wi da mortgage, but ... I tried ta tell her at I towt I might *pre-*

fer ta wirk on, if I could."

"She wid never understaand dat wan,"said her brother. "Wantin ta wirk, just for dee ain satisfaction, when doo hed an infant ta look efter – I don't tink she wid even mind doo ever said it."

She raised her head.

"I'm no criticisin dee, Chris. An God knows, I'm no really criticisin Mam edder. She just exasperates me dat much."

Years ago, Martin and she had been able to talk to each other. Then she had gone to university and he, who should have, refused, and somehow, awkwardness and then antagonism had grown between them. Something of their former closeness had suddenly returned. Christine realised, with a pang, how much she had missed it. Nobody, not even Jim, had replaced Martin. Nobody else shared the childhood years, the common ground.

He was moving round her kitchen, less unsteady now, finding cups, milk and biscuits. "Dere," he said, handing her a cup. "See what a liberated male I am."

"Does Mam ken doo can mak tay?" she asked, with a shaky smile.

He sat down by the table and began to eat a digestive biscuit. "Well," he said, "I ken at Africa exists, but I'm never seen it mesell. It's something da sam wi Mam an me an cookin of any kind. I made maet for six men tree times a day in twa year, but I'm never been allowed ta cook a meal in wir hoose. No if she's in."

Rain began to spatter the window. The kitchen felt warm and friendly, a homely sort of place on a rainy night. "I towt," said Christine, more relaxed now, "at Mam wid really *enjoy* keepin da baby, instead o bein on her own aa day. Does doo tink she just offered because she felt obleeged?"

"Weel, ta be honest, Chris, I wid a towt da sam as dee. It wis just at last week, Uncle Harry axed her if she wid laek ta come an wirk steady in da shop in da mornings. An she wis just aboot med up her mind ta go. An I towt, splendid, get her oot o da hoose among folk, an gie her something ta keep her lightsome. Just what she's needin. Dan doo comes along an we're back ta square wan!"

"I never kent! She never said ta me! I'll spaek tae her ageen."

"Chris," said Martin, offering her another biscuit, "doo needna budder. She's fairly decided. She's doin da right thing. Der naewye doo could affroad her noo. An lat's face it, she maybe only wanted da shop job tae obleege Uncle Harry. Foo wid we ever ken?"

They sat in silence for a little, listening to the rain. "Maybe it's da best at could happen," Martin said. "If Mam haes an infant ta fuss ower, she'll maybe no fuss ower me."

"It really gets tae dee dat bad?"

"It really maks me mad. Dan I get mad at mesell for gettin mad. It maks me hellish ill-natired."

The everyday began to look quite different. She had been too absorbed in her own busy life to see her family clearly. "Never ever doin anything just because she wanted tae. I never saw it laek dat afore." She looked at Martin. "Dat's terrible."

"It's no uncommon in weemen," he said. "Older weemen, anywye. Granny wis just da sam, I'm sure. Dey were brought up no ta tink aboot demsells, ta tink aboot idder folk first. Ta do what you ought ta do. Hit's dat deep athin dem at dey do it athoot tinkin at all. Christ, dere's Granny. walkin aroond on autopilot, no kennin day fae night an no kennin wha ta hell you are – but she'll still mak you welcome, an treat you laek royalty. Duty, bloody duty, still haes ta be done!"

"Is it no kindness?" asked Christine, almost in a whisper. "Dat's how *I* saw it. Nothing left o her but kindness." There was a note of pain, of pleading in the voice. "Doo's seein things awful black, Martin!"

"I tink too much." He looked away. Then he looked back at her and set down his cup. "Anywye," he said, "weemen is different noo. Aren' you?"

She was thinking. "Martin, it is possible I might no *want* ta go back ta wark. I'm no just fairly sure."

"Of coorse."

"It wid be ideal if I could wirk pairt-time."

"Oh great!" he said, shaking his head and smiling. "Dan doo could do *both* da things doo felt doo ought ta do! Magic!"

"Whan did doo turn intae a psychologist?" she queried, without resentment.

"Lass, it's winderful what six year at da fishing can do for you. Better as an honours degree." There was something in his voice...

"Why doesn't doo try da Open University?" she asked daringly.

Pause. "I'm towt aboot it. I might."

She was pleased, delighted, about to launch into encouragement and suggestions, till she saw the look in his eye.

"I *might*. An I might try ta win ta sea. An I might - I *will* - bigg a hoose ta mesell." He rose, looking down at her, again challenging. "An I might just drink mesell ta death. It's up ta me!"

"OK, OK, I get da message! Far be it fae me ta suggest at doo ought ta do anything!" She saw him to the door, again offering to drive him home, but he was determined to be unpredictable.

"I'll walk. Da rain is geen aff. I might as weel feel virtuous for wance." He grinned, and was gone, leaving her heartened, concerned and thoughtful, all at once.

The baby came home on a Saturday, visiting Agnes on her way.

"Lovely peerie lass! Lat me fin a penny ta gie her."

Babs stayed till teatime, and would have stayed longer.

"No, Mam, I'll be fine. Jim is here. Go doo home an do dee own wark. I'll be blyde ta see dee da moarn."

"Weel, if doo's sure..." A quick visit from Martin before bedtime.

"She's lovely, Chris. I'll no hadd her, no, I'm aa cement. Got me foond feenished da night."

Jim poured a celebration dram. The baby lay half-asleep and contented, a bundle of tiny perfections, a curled ball of instinct, potential and personality unknown. "Modern woman, Mark Two," said her uncle. "Here's tae her."

Reviews

Cabaret McGonagall, W.N. Herbert, Bloodaxe Books, £7.95; *Red Letter Day*, Tom Pow, Bloodaxe Books, £7.95; *Histories of Desire*, Ron Butlin, Bloodaxe Books, £6.95; *Masculinity*, Robert Crawford, Cape Poetry, £7.00; *The Devil in the Driving Mirror*, Peter McCarey, Vennel Press, £6.99; *Sheet Mettle*, Drew Milne, Alfred David Editions, £6.50.

The jacket of *Cabaret McGonagall* calls Herbert "a highly versatile poet" and this collection is indeed various if nothing else. If I state at the outset that I found the book uneven, I hope it will be clear that I mean it contains both powerful and mature pieces of work (often with a liberal dose of wit) as well as somewhat slighter writing. This very unevenness may well be due to the breadth of styles, forms and voices Herbert has attempted in this patchwork quilt of a book – a risk worth taking for any poet and one which many of Herbert's contemporaries shy away from

One of the problems I have with some of the poems is that sometimes ideas from Herbert's very inventive imagination become the medium of the poem instead of language itself. Obviously a poetry entirely lacking in imagination is one of poverty, but equally it should arise from an interest in the working of language, rather than subjugate that necessity of poetry to its own demands. When Herbert's associative method is at its most surreal, there is a mixing of concrete and abstract which to my mind only weakens his otherwise deft presentation of precise and keenly-observed details. This is perhaps an inevitability of surrealism and those who prize the function of the subconscious above the function of language will not share my complaint. "The King and Queen of Dumfriesshire" is a case in point. The masterful image of a couple "...cast in bronze, with Henry Moore holes/shot in each other..." is appended with the redundant "by incessant argument;". The following lines from the same poem contain an interesting idea:

On the back seat rests
Their favourite argument, the one about
how he does not permit her to see the old friends
she no longer likes and he secretly misses;
the one which is really about punishing each other
for no longer wanting to make love.

The argument is in the form of a big white bowl with a black band around it hand-painted with fruit.

The execution of the idea seems clumsy, both in its prosaic phrasing and the heavy-handed exposition of the meaning of the lines (to be fair, the next six lines of the same poem are tauter and more memorable in their precision). Elsewhere, Herbert is too willing to allow discursive fillers to mediate between the reader and the poem and undermine the experience being presented (see "The Postcards of Scotland").

When writing to tighter stanza forms, fewer of these distractions are given space and the writing really takes off. In poems like "The Flock in the Firth" and "Ballad of the New King's Dialect" language is in part the poem's subject as well as medium and ideas are discharged almost effortlessly from these well-wrought poem-machines. These and other of Herbert's Scottish poems ("The Ballad of the Hermit Crab" and "August in the Laich") really sing and it is tempting to conclude that the poet finds his true voice in that language rather than English. The lovely "Smirr" and the long, loping, Ginsbergian movement to "Becoming Joseph" prove this to be a dangerous generalisation to make.

Drew Milne is quite a different kind of poet. Herbert complains in "Ballad of a Failure";

For seven years I tried to make
the abstract surface sing,
and never found a reader who'd
admit they'd heard a thing.

Milne *is* a poet whose surface sings and this is at least one reader who hears something of that music. Milne delights in the texture of words, and tortures and teases syntax in pursuit of a disjunctive, but sparkling music. There are similarities between his method and that of the American L.A.N.G.U.A.G.E poets, yet he is never as abstruse as that group.

The surface is not the only layer of interest however; rather an idea of 'normal' language structure is present throughout the verse and Milne's subversions of this idea set up a creative friction. Words *do* have their referential values as well as physical, acoustic properties and the reader is invited to tease a 'sense' reading from them in addition to sounding their music. The book explicitly demands an active participation of its audience and playfully welcomes the curious reader. Milne takes up Cummings' exhortation "sharpen say to sing" and fulfils it admirably. However, there is not merely an attractive aesthetic at work here. Many poems show a keen political awareness and strong sense of social commitment. The poems have such a cohesive integrity that it is hard to illustrate my point with short quotations. "Through the Buy-out Jargon" is a particularly fine example, as is "The Idea of Order at Habermas-Platz". Also worthy of mention is the moving and intimate sequence of love poems, "A Garden of Tears" – nine poems written in something very similar to sonnet form.

Peter McCarey has a good ear for subtle and effective rhythms and one is always aware of the forward momentum of the prosody driving on the development of the poem's matter. *The Devil in the Driving Mirror* is an intriguing sequence in which a certain 'Hatchek' undertakes a kind of magic-realist journey through a variety of landscapes and periods, accompanied by a robot and golem.

To my ear Eliot haunts the whole book. A number of specific scenes are surely conscious (too self-conscious?) echoes of *The Waste Land* (for example the tarot-reader in the first section, or the carpet dealer in the hotel "They dealt in execrable French/and execrated English."). More usefully McCarey has appropriated Eliot's ability to integrate colloquial speech and dialogue into passages of greater intensity and lyricism. This is not to say his technique of composition is at all fragmentary; rather the opposite. Shifts in time and place happen almost imperceptibly. One scene blurs into another and the whole is a surprisingly convincing, unified narrative structure. Story-telling – the constant unfolding of a plot (as opposed to theme development), is not an art now commonly associated with poetry, having for the most part been surrendered to the novel some time ago. McCarey rescues it with this beautiful blend of the real and non-real, and offers a helpful model to any poet considering narrative.

It would be unfair to leave this book without noting the beautiful vowel music that McCarey deploys across some passages. This, from the first section, should serve as an illustration:

Hatchek didn't answer him, but said:

I worked in a condemned and listed
greenhouse, growing coleus
I had to souse with nicotine,
and all that kept me breathing
was the draft across space
where elephatine palms had prised from astragals
plates of glass that changed and spangled or
came to rest on bended stems, and...Ah
but there's the man I'm looking for.
Doctor Meyrink!

Robert Crawford's book divides into four parts, the poems in each linked by a common theme. Parts of the book tend towards the anecdotal and are sometimes unremarkable. Memories are recalled and recorded, which, as Thom Gunn once asserted, is the first impulse that drives the poet to write. Sometimes a detail is vividly caught, but rarely does an entire poem project itself off the page. Perhaps I have the section "Growing" uppermost in mind. There is a lot of this kind of poetry about (dealing with childhood memories) and eventually one's receptiveness to more of it is blunted. Apart from the wit and verve of "Chaps" and the pair of 'Helicopter' poems in the title-section, it is not until the third section ("Scotch Broth") that very much exciting happens.

Here the book seems to suddenly change gear. It's by no means a safe postulation to make, but maybe Crawford is more engaged with his subject (Scotland) in this section. Something, in any case, animates these lines, which start to sing more than the earlier parts.

Images are effective both conceptually, and because of the words those concepts are bound up in. To single out one poem is again difficult. The whole of "Carpet" is outstanding, but the juxtaposition of images at the end is particularly memorable:

A pretty, stockinged, telephoning lady.
One silver paperclip dangles from the carpet's edge.

"Ballad" also exhibits this sharpness and there is a great Whitman parody ("Consumptive"), which demonstrates admiration for the poet, as well as having its tongue slightly in cheek. The whole section attempts to 'say' little about Scotland. The "I" of the author is present less than elsewhere in the volume and often only introduces a poem. Yet without trying, the sequence celebrates, raises questions, laments, criticizes and records modern Scottish society and its relation to its own past and future more interestingly and honestly than any amount of authorial comment would have otherwise done.

Space does not permit me to say very much about Tom Pow's or Ron Butlin's books. That being the case, I'll attempt only to highlight a few of the positive aspects of each poet's work.

Pow has a gift for evoking the atmosphere of a place quite vividly, even for a reader who has never had experience of the places in question. He has indeed published a book of travel writing and this collection can in part be thought of as travel poetry. Part of his success at presenting details lies in the way in which an experience grounded in one of the physical senses often leads to, or is described through, another of the senses. This creates a richly sensual texture to the poems. These lines from "Last Night in the Tropics" describe a bat;

I trace its flight
back to the deepest crush
of blue-blackness. Smells
of ginger and garlic
drift round the wall
from where light licks
into the darkness.

At times Pow employs subtle assonance and half-rhyme, which, together with a restrained use of enjambement lend the verse a pleasing lilt ("Coda: Lament" and "In the Botanics: Edinburgh" are further good examples).

Butlin is not a poet who sings very much, rather he offers the reader intimate vignettes and cameos. A strong, personal affiliation with place is apparent from these poems and often passion for a lover seems inseparable from passion for place ("The Lake at Preda" for example). Butlin is at his best when he writes epigrammatically. The economy of "One Life" demonstrates this and is as good a poem to finish with as any other from these volumes;

1
Once when I was young I reached into the fire from longing to possess the colours there.

2
I am the fire I'm reaching into now.
I grasp at flames and burn:
I am the colours that one by one return.

Chris Jones

Theatre Roundup
All singing, all dancing academics

George Steiner caused a furore in this year's Edinburgh Festival Lecture by telling us that science has now seized the high ground of human intellectual endeavour, leaving the arts floundering and looking irreverently self-indulgent. Some of his argument stemmed from the improbable statistic that 90% of all scientists are alive today, and *they* are on the upward escalator, us artists, presumably, on the black treadmill to limbo. Quoting the Edinburgh Provost hailing the first Festival in 1947, as "A Festival to embrace the world!", Steiner added, "The object of that affection has hardly matched his largess." Well, how could we expect it to! You don't neglect the bairn further just because it is a bit stoorie.

To make us feel better he made some sycophantic remarks about Scotland:

> One of the disabling weaknesses of current Western literature is its unwillingness or inability to engage with the dance of the spirit in the sciences. Music and the arts are equipped to do better. The native land of Watt and of Kelvin, of Maxwell and of Faraday, could give a lead.

Well, maybe we could – indeed, already have! In the land of Kelvin, arts and sciences are more inclined to walk hand in hand, without indulging in demeaning platitudes about each others' contribution to the welfare of humanity.

Having stalked the streets almost 24 hours a day during the Festival, it has to be said that all of human life was there, including science. This may be through the medium of drama, music, art, dance, discussion, or just the extra-intense pub conversations late into the night. Taking the Festival as a whole, it cannot be dismissed as an elitist self-indulgence. There was no escape, for example, from the terrible problems of Bosnia, or Africa, or Scotland for that matter. All these had a presence.

Steiner quoted Auden's complaint that "poems make nothing happen", without stopping to think that science, ungoverned by any sensible system of values related to human needs, may make too much happen too quickly. Greater dialogue between arts and sciences is of course desireable, and each has something unique to contribute. The problem is when one becomes isolated from the other.

One thing might stick from Steiner's rather pompous and confused speech – Edinburgh could create a special slot where the problem of communication between these endeavours is addressed. Professor Davies from Adelaide, suggested that the Science Festival be relocated into the Festival, which would not be a good thing. Edinburgh in August groans with Festivals. We could, however, take a lead in hosting a series of events where the Film Festival comes out of its movie bubble, theatre sees the Book Festival and the arts the sciences. Scientists complain that artists like Fay Weldon say stupid things about them and their work, but Steiner is guilty of perpetuating the same nonsense, in elevating science at the expense of the arts. The best artists are only too keen to know what's happening on the frontiers of science, and the best scientists want to discover what these anarchic artists are on about. That's how it must be, and the backwoodsmen on both sides shouldn't be taken seriously.

To come down to specifics, the official Festival programme is in danger of being too staid, insufficiently committed to the new and challenging. The music programme was conservative beyond belief, up to your oxters in Brahms and Hayden, with the possible exception of James MacMillan's *Ines de Castro* which the English critics (of course) didn't like. I am told the Nederlands Dans Theater was wonderful, but maybe it's time Brian McMaster omitted Mark Morris from the line-up. Opera-wise *Orfeo ed Euridice* was indifferently sung and badly staged ("Out of Gluck" one critic unkindly said.) But this is where it gets difficult. Mark Morris's dancers did passably well in *Orfeo*, but so scunnered were many by the thought of another Gluck that they simply couldn't face going to *Iphigenie auf Tauris* for more of that classical crap. But there is a difference between Mark Morris and Pina Bausch (although I thought her production last year *Carnations* pretentious and thin). Bausch's *Iphigenie* was the perfect retort to Professor Steiner, demonstrating that, age-old though its theme and something of a classical standby, performed with enough commitment and imagination, it is as relevant today as ever. But the Festival has to be seen to

be artistically adventurous, and juxtaposing the two Glucks in the same Festival was not a good idea. There were adventurous things though, and I suppose Houston Grand Opera's *Four Saints in Three Acts* (Gertrude Stein) fell into that category, but it was that rarified kind of *avant-garde* with a message that would fit comfortably onto a postage stamp. I didn't last half an hour. But, unexpectedly, *Der Rosenkavalier* a silent film played to live music, was one of the most diverting experiences of the Festival. I will never again see that opera without giggling at the memory of this ruthlessly funny send-up.

The drama this year was disappointing. Not having Robert Lepage's *Elsinore* was a major letdown, *Orlando* was beautiful to look at but nothing to write home about and *Time and the Room,* supposedly exposing us to the work of one of Europe's most controversial playwrights, Botho Strauss, was a depressingly predictable experience. It might have made more impact if performed with irreverant panache, by the like of Hull Truck Theatre, or with the classical style of the Citz. As it was, it was Ayckbourn in a mood of waggish surrealism, but without much to say.

By contrast, the Catalan play *L'esplèndida vergonya del fet mal fet* by Carlos Santos was anarchically stupendous. It didn't matter what it was about (something to do with Christopher Columbus) but so engagingly imaginative was the performance and production as sheer spectacle that it didn't matter a damn. It was raunchy, acrobatic, energetic, giving two fingers to all dramatic and musical conventions (for at least five minutes one actor played the violin splendidly upside down hanging onto a rope with his feet). On the more conventional side, we anticipated four hours of Teatra di Roma's *Uncle Vanya* with grim foreboding, but it was quite brilliant. The Italians brought such grace and style to it, exposing the emotions of the play as perhaps only Italians could. A Russian treatment might be too ponderous, an English one too formal and clinical. Peter Stein's genius as a director is to turn a play inside out, expose its innards to liberate the playwright's intentions, and then let it breath. It takes time, but the result is mesmerising.

Some trends emerge here: Brian McMaster keeps some of the best cards up his sleeve to stun us at the end when we're nearly off our feet with exhaustion. Some productions which look drearily boring turn out to be a pleasing surprise, and the so-called *avant-garde* cutting edge is discovered to be dully predictable. McMaster is tending to repeat himself - Mark Morris, Pina Bausch, Beethoven. Clearly there is a Scottish problem: there isn't enough there he tends to go for something safe. John McGrath's *Satire of the Four Estaites* was enjoyable, but too focussed on the media as the root of all evil, and the script full of rather lazy jokes. In the end, I warmed to it, but it missed so many opportunities for biting satire *à la* David Lyndsay – in particular the magnificent John the Commonweal speech, and generally was just too soap-operatic. You can virtually depend on it that the English critics won't like whatever Scottish plays are showcased on the Festival, so McMaster can actually afford more to throw fortune to the winds.

Steiner's *coup de grâce* was the following, oxymoronic observation: "To know when to stop is a rare but vivid mark of honesty within excellence". This is like telling someone that they're so fine at 50 they should make sure to shuffle off their mortals now. Yes, of course, the Festival must change. But to bring down the Curtain on such a magnificent success, taking the Festival as a whole, the vibrant Fringe (a bewildering plenitude of material) the Fireworks, for which virtually the entire population of Edinburgh turns out, the sheer Street Theatre of a cosmopolitan population rubbing shoulders with each other within the relatively constricted confines of Edinburgh, it is a unique world phenomenon. Its long-standing success, quite apart from the excellence or otherwise of the art it features, is, I'm sure, down to the intimate, villagey nature of Edinburgh. Somehow it manages to absorb this massive invasion without losing this village character. That's why that the most powerful method of publicity is the hyperactive grapevine, which works because people talk to each other all over the place, within a relatively small geographical area dominated by cluttered mediaeval architecture. To stop all this now would not be an act of honesty, as Steiner has it, but an act of cultural vandalism for which the world would never forgive us.

Joy Hendry

Pamphleteer

In his poem 'With Thanks and Homage to that Critic' Gael Turnbull is advised by an unknown literary critic to

> keep out of the salt
> swamps of literature and live
> on your own rocky island
> with a lake and a spring on it.

Most of the writers in this Pamphleteer are acting contrary to this mystical critic's advice. In order to find an audience in the 'literary world', that is too say, attain that Holy Grail and get published; more and more writers are leaving the safety of their private worlds of poetry and turn to small presses and self-publication. There is only a small audience for these and little money to be made but authors and publishers risk their own little islands to wander out into the fiercer world of literature.

Gael Turnbull is a fine example of this. His book *To the Tune of Annie Laurie* is full of short, often humorous, thought-provoking poems. I was disappointed though; I felt they lacked substance and only touched on her subjects which range from Calvinism to skylights. His voice is intriguing but he didn't go far enough. To the Tune of Annie Laurie is available from Akros, 65 Warrender Park Terrace, Edinburgh at £2.15.

Three new debut works from Crocus, Commonwealth Ltd., Cheetwood House, 21 Newton Street, Manchester M1 1FZ: *Regrouting the Bathroom in the Wrong Century* by Alan Peat, *Art is only a Boy's Name* by Liz Almond and *Life's a Tupperware Party* by Mandy Precious all selling at £2.50.

I couldn't really get into Alan Peat's poems despite his amazing range of vocabulary that made each piece a puzzle to solve; "Their ossiferous closets," "A Sisyphean wish to sleep,/The obsessive reading of encapsulated fire regulations." Maybe these puzzles were too much for me.

Yet I genuinely enjoyed Liz Almond's book. It contained beautifully woven images in unexpected settings. Her language has a kind of power that is not lost but strengthened by the excellent imagery. In the poem 'Tiananmen' she says

'If you want to know the taste of a pear You must change the pear by eating it.'

So she took up her paring knife
And made the rosy skin fall in a coil
Exposing flesh bloated by fruit sugar

Mandy Precious' poems look at the less than pretty side of life with a gentle but critical touch whether it is a woman who has lived her entire life in institutions or children making fun of a girl whose brother has just died. At times, however, the language is weak and unable to give the poems the support their powerful subjects need.

Spout Publications at Birstall Library, Market Street, Birstall, Batley, West Yorks WF17 9EN has also come out with three new selections of poetry. The first group of poems in Susannah White's *Shall I?* £2.50 looks at the everyday world from a different angle, using her surreal imagery to illustrate her themes as in 'Her Husband Has Two Heads' and 'Whatever'. The later poems in the collection focus on being a housewife and mother. Her lack of punctuation works here as it suggests grocery lists or lists of things to do.

towels smell
damp
bathroom
blisters paint
milk plops
into coffee.

The long title poem in *Dancing Fish* by Michael Wilkinson £4 works nature together with human emotion. It moves between figures, images, voices until it is only the starkness of the landscape and the emotion that comes through strongly.

Our final Spout publication is *Tin Cat Alley* by Mark Murphy £4. I enjoyed his poems on the subjects of famous paintings. An Edwardian model dreams of being taken, another talks back to Modigliani about adultery – they reveal the hidden undercurrents in all forms of arts. What was going on behind the scenes puts listening to music, reading or even watching a film in a new light for me.

Claiming "Believed to be the first collection of its kind" Bruce Leeming's *Scots Haiku* is a refreshing read. Published by Hub Editions, Church Road, Terrington, St. John, Cambs. PE14 7SS at £3 it contains haiku in Lallans with English translations. Using the Scottish landscape as palette the poems are elegantly simple, creating a snapshot of a moment.

Heich i' the corries
snaw: doon here het sin
– kye doverin

In the high corries
snow: down here hot sun
– cattle dozing.

Even if your Lallans is not that proficient, like my own, the English translations make the Scots accessible.

Markings: New Writing and Art from Dumfries and Galloway published by Forward Press, Castle Douglas at £1.50 offers local writers and artists a chance to exhibit their work. Issues 1 and 2 (Summer 1995 and Winter 1995/6) prove that the area has talented individuals to put on show. The subjects are far ranging and often topical. It is a good place for new writers to make a start.

Moving onto Dundee, in particular Anna MacDonald who has self-published several children's books: *Clifton and Friends, More About Clifton and Friends* and *A Handful of Limericks and Nonsense Verse for Schools*. The Clifton Books are about Clifton Tortoise and his animal friends. Written in simple verse they are excellent to read to small children; older ones will soon lose interest in the line drawings and basic adventures. I found the nonsense verse book basically unhumerous and many of the limericks just did not seem to scan well so that they read uncomfortably.

Another children's book also in verse, but this time in Scots is *The Wild Haggis and the Greetin-faced Nyaff* by Stewart McHardy at £4.95 from the Scottish Children's Press. "The three-leggit Haggis is a gey oorie burd;/ ae short leg, twa lang anes an luiks just absurd." "The Nyaff is a teeny wee thing like a flea/ sae scrunchit an shilpit he's real hard tae see." This book is excellent for those who wish to keep Scots alive in their children and to show them that it is not just a verbal dialect. I found myself wondering, though, why the blurb is written in English.

Fuck Scotland by Francis Gallagher – F.G. Publications, 36 Mavis Bank Gardens, Bellshill, ML4 3ES £4 is a shock for anyone going by just the title. It is a barrage of emotion and straight-shooting language, but not just a rant. Gallagher manages to expose his view of real-life Scotland (I won't say working-class as it is one of his targets). He points out what he sees as problems, but is willing to offer solutions. "Scotland's in no man's land the past/ cannot be continued/ future can't be reached so the stagnant drag/ the longevity of the ruined." His lack of punctuation and capitalisation often makes following his train of thought difficult but it does give the effect of emotion and energy spilling out.

This issue's selection from Smith/Doorstep Books includes *My Sister's Horse* by Selima Hill, *The Boy on the Edge of Happiness* by Matthew Hollis, *The Sandfield's Baudelaire* by Stephen Knight and *The Mammoth's Knee* by Sue Butler. They are all priced at £2.95.

Stephen Knight's poems are written in phonetic using numbers and parts of recognizable words to make it the most unreadable Scots I have ever come across. Listening to them without looking at the puzzling signs and thinking about what they said proved an easier way to decipher them. Still it was too much effort.

I liked Matthew Hollis' collection of poems from the standpoint of famous composers' wives and lovers such as 'Nocturen' about Chopin. I wished they were a little more musical to keep them in contact with their themes but they are touching and original.

Sue Butler's *The Mammoth's Knee* is full of sumptuous detail as in the poem 'Being Drawn' "In her pores, the fetid/animal breath of the Metro; the ellipse of evacuee glasses/ is reflected in the samovar." The pictures her words paint are personal and revealing, seeming to hide references from us, but drawing us on to discover their meanings.

My Sister's Horse illustrates facets of the relationship between sisters. Hat and kittens abound but I never got to know either girl or how they viewed each other. Turning to each poem individually was more satisfactory than the collection as a related piece.

This is a small choice of the books that ought to be introduced to the public. Poetry is obviously not dead but moving out to the masses in a quiet manner with plenty of reputable small presses to lend a helping hand.

Gerry Stewart

Catalogue

Scottish traditional music is more alive today than it was before the hype of popular music. *The Nineties Collection: New Scottish Tunes in Traditional Style* (£12.99) launched by TMSA gives us proof of this fact. Composers as young as eleven sent in nearly 400 tunes, half of which are compiled here. This makes it a book to be used, not put on the shelf. For those who'd like to listen but not actually play the fiddle, pipe, accordion or harp the same pieces of music are recorded by Greentrax on CD and cassette.

Another sign of the popularity of traditional music is the publication of *Piobaireachd And Its Interpretation: Classical Music Of The Highland Bagpipe* (£15). The late Seumas MacNeill, Principal of the College of Piping, and Frank Richardson (twice winner of the "Royal Scottish Piper Society' Piobaireachd" Competition) have collected information on the historical development of pipes, the description of Piobaireachd and the masters at playing this very elaborate kind of music. They also give guidelines for listening to and understanding this special way of playing the bagpipes. Thus the book allows adepts and amateurs alike to learn about a rather exclusive subject.

A booklet that requires few words of introduction is *The Scottish Folk Directory '96*. Published for the first time 30 years ago, it has been around ever since. It advertises storytellers, ceilidh bands, other musicians, tutors, etc. If you want harp lessons or you wish to bring out your first record it is worth while looking at the Directory. It also provides information on what's on in the world of folk which gives it a wider audience appeal as well.

Anyone who wants to dive into the depths of the heroic Celtic past should own the following book published by EUP. *The Poems of Ossian and Related Works* (£16.95) contains not only poems about Fingal and Temora, but also "Fragments of Ancient Poetry" and some contemporary critical work. This publication may attract readers who want to know about Macpherson's falsification of old Celtic mythology, and to see him re-established as a man of merit who preserved old manuscripts from being lost forever. It also provides "a reliable text" which the editor, Howard Gaskill, points out has been rather difficult so far. The painstaking work he put into this is obvious: more than a hundred pages of annotations and a helpful register of names ease and complete your reading.

Editor Derick S. Thomson arouses a lot of curiosity in his introduction to Alasdair Mac Mhaighstir Alasdair: *Selected Poems* (Scottish Academic Press, £11.50), when he says the poems contain "excessive descriptions of Nature and poems brimming over with phantastic ideas". The book contains a collection of Gaelic political and satirical verse as well as drinking songs. Its introduction provides detailed information about Mac Mhaighsitr Alasdair's life in the 18th century, about the vocabulary of his time and the author's poetry in general. The list of references mentioned and the short forward to each poem makes it excellent for academic work.

Edinburgh University Press launched their Centenary Edition to mark the 100th anniversary of R.L. Stevenson's death, formatting all of his work into a new and well-crafted shape. The editors – Peter Hinchcliffe and Catherine Kerrigan – were noticably concerned with creating "good books" which could be used by students and ordinary people alike. They included an large number of helpful notes on a variety of background knowledge. The books on review are the well-known *Weir Of Hermiston* and *The Ebb Tide*. The latter is part of Stevenston's more phantastic South Sea writing, yet it contains a strong vein of realism which left Stevenson's original editor at first rather reluctant to publish it.

Another planned set of classics from Edinburgh University Press is Sir Walter Scott's works in 30 volumes within the next 10 years. Two of them have recently appeared on the market: *The Bride of Lammermoor* and *A Legend Of The Wars Of Montrose*. The editor J.H. Alexander may pride himself with having published an edition which is free of former errors, with an index of quotations and their sources and with issuing the original text that Scott created for his reader.

Three Go Back by Lewis Grassic Gibbon is a distracting book and can incite your imagination to create stories of its own, taking you beyond the author's own ideas (Polygon; £7.99). In it we come across three time-travellers from the 1930's, who take us back 25000 years to a handsome, hospitable tribe of Cro-Magnards who roamed Southern France and the Basque Country. *Three Go Back* is an absorbing novel which asks "What if we could

change our own history?". Its strength lies in its language, not so much in its plot, even the biggest problem – the return to the 20th century – is resolved simply. What is most striking is the fact that this sci-fi novel was written in the 1930s but hasn't lost any of its validity: The three protagonists represent three different concepts of morality which still struggle against each other today.

Just Duffy is for the serious-minded (Canongate Classics, £4.99). Duffy is believed to be "a bit funny in the head" by most people because of his preoccupation with the truth. The sixteen year old – disgusted by the (religious) hypocrisy of the world surrounding him – tries to get to the bottom of it all by declaring war on all those institutions and people whom he holds responsible for the state of things. Although this novel by Robin Jenkins is highly recommended as "one of the most important of recent Scottish novels", for its dealing of the question of good and evil, it is bound to put quite a few readers off as it utterly lacks humour. Both the novel and protagonist are so sour and moralising that being bad seems to offer more fun in life than being virtuous.

Carcanet has recently published poetry from two men of great renown. *Collected Poems* by Iain Crichton Smith (£9.95) has been honoured with the "Poetry Book Society Special Commendation Saltire Prize". It follows the poet's development from 1955 to 1979. Iain Crichton Smith is a master at describing ordinary people's lives in words that are neither trivial nor difficult to comprehend. His poetry bears witness to his Scottish origin, yet at the same time it reaches further than that, relating to people outside Scotland.

Edwin Morgan's *Collected Poems* (£14.95) comprises poems from 1949 to 1987, revealing a versatile writer: Morgan moves from the concrete to a more classical poetic style, and never allows us forget the 20th century. Yet in comparison to Iain Crichton Smith – if they may be compared at all — his poems don't read easily. Some of them seem rather intellectual, if not artificial, and difficult to understand; they are certainly not suited for "having a quick glance at" and they require a curious reader.

Another work by Iain Crichton Smith has been recorded on cassette by Canongate Audio. *Consider The Lilies* tells of an old woman, who is compelled to leave the house she was born in. This causes her to look back on her unidyllic life. This unexpected event gives her existence an unexpected turn and makes the charming story exciting

Useful for less experienced writers than Morgan and Smith is *Metre, Rhythm and Verse Form* (Routledge) a book for students, but also for anyone who wishes to speak intelligently about poetry. Philip Hobsbaum, Professor of English Literature at Glasgow University, gives qualified explanations on technical terms like 'prosody', 'rhythm' or 'jambus' and gives numerous examples to clarify his definitions.

Aspiring writers should also note the two following titles which may not catapult them into fame, but might help them find out about the basics of authorship. A classic in this "business" is Dorothea Brande's *Becoming A Writer* (Macmillan, £9.99). It was originally written in 1934 and has been in demand ever since. There is not much you can add to Malcolm Bradbury's introduction: this book doesn't simply give you rules to abide by, it gives you an individual, friendly and psychological way of tackling the how, what and when of writing.

The Writer's Companion by Barry Turner completes Brande's guidelines. This publication provides answers to numerous questions such as how do you find the right media for your writing , how to find the best publisher, how to sell your article or book and how to finance your writing? It also gives you answers to legal questions and a lot of practical detailed information about the business side of writing.

"This is the book they told us we shouldn't write." – This is no quotation from any writers' handbook but from a publication on Scotland at its worst - appropriately titled *Scotland The Worst!* (Canongate, £4.99). It promises some fun and indeed tales of the worst ...it makes you chuckle, yet you won't crack up laughing. It may be a nice little present.

A dearer gift for dearer people could be Behind The Facade (HMSO) - after all it costs £25.00. Starting in the Renaissance it tells the story of 400 years of Scottish interiors, important architects and a bit about history, and all illustrated by photographs of buildings and furniture. Anyone looking for the interior of modest accommodation will search for it in vain in Sheila Mackay's book.

Margarete Weber

Southfields

volume one
> The Literary Thirties: Scottish perspectives

> *Edwin Morgan*: photocopy art

> The Queen of Sheba is alive and well and living in Fife

volume two
> The poet that Greenock Shut Up

> Earthquakes - *by Victor Serge*

> News fae a Derk Corner of Britayne

Southfields is full of poetry, essays, visuals, and fiction. It's over 180 pages fat, and costs £7 a throw. Cheques to: Southfields Press, 8 Richmond Rd Staines, Middlesex TW18 2AB.

Oxford Quarterly Review

Issue One features new poetry from Les Murray, Michael S. Weaver, Shanta Acharya, Mario Petrucci, and an essay on film montage by David Mamet.

Issue Two features new poetry from seven Pulitzer Prize-winners (Caroline Kizer, Anthony Hecht, W.D. Snodgrass, Galway Kinnell, Jorie Graham, Charles Simic, and Charles Wright), Edwin Morgan, Ian Hamilton, Miles Champion, and first-time translations of top Polish and Rumanian poets.

Issue Three, appearing in December, will include new work from Donald Justice, Adrienne Rich, Philip Levine, Louise Glück, James Dickey, and Christopher Middleton.

U.K. subscription,
£20 Institutional
£16 Individual

From: *Oxford Quarterly Review*,
St. Catherine's College,
Oxford OX1 3UJ, UK

Notes on Contributors

George Bruce: these poems render biographical detail unnecessary, but I wish it to be known that my Uncle, Francis George Scott, generally punctilious in his dress had been in debate with me until 5am

Jim Brunton: Leither (so motto "Perservere"); Heriot's, Edinburgh University; soldier, tram conductor, civil servant. Now retired, is a periodic features contributor to the *Scotsman*. Has always written poems – slowly improving.

Bernadette Maria Creechan works in a library. Poetry and fiction published in Britain, Australia and S. Africa. Theatre: 1993 Young Scottish Playwrights Festival, Mayfest 1995, TIE play (Borderline Theatre 1994).

Yvonne D Claire is Swiss, was joint winner of the Edinburgh Review 10th Anniversary Short Story Competition. She lives in Edinburgh with her husband & their dog.

James Deahl: one part Welshman, one part Scot, born in the USA (like Bruce Springsteen, but lives in Canada. Author of a dozen books, all worth reading. Almost met Hugh MacDiarmid once.

Jenni Daiches writes biography and literary and social history as Jenni Calder. Her first collection if poetry, *Mediterranean*, was published by the Scottish Cultural Press.

Garry Egan: formerly an adult literacy tutor, not a trainee accountant, and now is a full-time freelance writer.

Owen Gallagher: from Glasgow now lives in London. Poems in *Verse, Gairfish, Lines Review* etc. Seeking a publisher for his first collection.

John Hamilton: born Zambia 1958. Brought up in Co Derry. Now works with his wife making jewellery in the Borders. Tells stories on the folk music scene.

Chris Harvie was born in 1944, grew up in the Scottish Borders, and graduated from Edinburgh University He is now Professor of British & Irish Studies at the University of Tübingen.

WN Herbert: latest book, *Cabaret McGonagall* is available from Bloodaxe. He is currently Northern Arts Literary Fellow at the Newcastle & Durham Universities, but will be north of the border again as soon as a large denomination bill is wafted under his nose.

Brent Hodgson: born New Zealand c. 1845!

Submits poetry & fiction to literary outlets regularly as the sight of a postman makes with an empty sack makes him go doo-lally

Eliza Langland is a Scottish based actress and writer.

Laureen Johnson: belongs to Shetland. Contributes to *New Shetlander* magazine. Stories also in *Northwords* and *A Tongue in Yer Heid* (B &W).

Chris Jones studied in London and Belfast. Now lives in Oxford and teaches English as a foreign language. writes and performs poetry, co-edits the magazine *Symtex & Grimmer*.

Peter McCarey: poetry includes *Town Shanties* (Broch Books) and *Tantris* (first part published in the Arvon Poetry Prizewinners' Anthology). Paludrine is an antimalarial drug; both D and MacD had malaria ...

David Mackenzie comes from Easter Ross. he is the author of one novel, *The Truth of Stone*, and several stories, one of which – "Photogenic" – Appeared in *Chapman* 53.

aonghas macneacail: born on the Isle of Skye in 1942. Much anthologized Gaelic & English poet, broadcaster, scriptwriter, journalist etc. *Rock and Water* published by Polygon.

Donald S Murray formerly lived on Lewis, where many shared his surname and forename. After moving south to Benbecula, he is now much easier to find in the telephone directory.

William Neill: poet, and translator, in Scots, Gaelic and English. Born Ayrshire, 1922. SAC Book Award Winner. *Selected Poems 1969-92* published by Cannongate.

Heather Reyes currently lives in Essex, dividing her time between teaching and research at London University, writing and her family. Has published short fiction, poetry and children's stories.

Gerry Stewart is an American living and studying in Glasgow. She has recently returned from teaching English in Greece.

Margarette Weber studies English Literature at the München Universität. She has travelled in Europe, spending some time as a Chapman volunteer.

Hamish Wallochie is a pedantic old git who will argue the toss about the orthographics of the Doric or a recipe for tablet at a meeting of the Scots Language Society.